Dive! Dive! Dive!

A Sport Divers' Guide

David Hodgson

Dive! Dive! Dive!

A Sport Divers' Guide

'Would'st thou.'—so the helmsman answered,
'Learn the secret of the sea?'
'Only those who brave its dangers
Comprehend its mystery!'

Longfellow—The Secret of the Sea

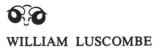

WILLIAM LUSCOMBE

First published in Great Britain by
William Luscombe Publisher Limited
Artists House
14 Manette Street
London W1V 5LB
1975

ISBN 0 86002 053 3

Text set in 11 pt. Photon Times, printed by photolithography, and bound in Great Britain at The Pitman Press, Bath

To all divers whose skill and courage have added to our knowledge and understanding of the world beneath the waves this book is dedicated . . .

Acknowledgements

Many divers and friends around the world have helped in the preparation of this book—to all of them my sincere thanks. I am especially grateful to Chez and Margot Parker, Council Members of the British Sub Aqua Club, and to Alan Bax and Jim Gill of Fort Bovisand for their time and trouble in checking sections of the manuscript, although of course any errors or opinions in this book are my own.

I am also very grateful to Mrs Margaret Rule of the Council for Nautical Archaeology for her help and advice, and to Colin Martin of the Institute of Maritime Archaeology, St Andrews, Scotland and the Council of Nautical Archaeology for permission to quote from his report on the Santa Maria de la Rosa expedition (CNA Newsletter No. 4). My thanks also to H. L. Blackmore, Keeper of Firearms at the Tower of London and Mr Austin Carpenter of the Department of the Environment. Flip Schulke of Miami, Florida was kind enough to provide help and advice and allow me permission to use certain technical information first published in the December 1973 issue of the *Journal of the SMPTE* (82nd Vol.), Peter Salmon of Aquamatic was also kind enough to provide valuable technical information relating to the construction of underwater housings.

I am indebted to the British Sub Aqua Club's Director General, Reg Vallintine and to the members of Number One Branch for their help in preparing some of the illustrations for this book, and I would particularly like to thank Ed Wilman the Branch Chairman. Mr Bernard Eaton, Editor of *Triton* and the *Diver* magazines was good enough to provide help and advice in the early planning stages of this book. Mr A. C. Tillbrook, managing director of A. Tillbrook and Co. Ltd, and Subaqua Services (Equipment) Ltd provided useful technical information about diving equipment.

Information about diving around the world was provided by diving enthusiasts and experts in the countries concerned. My thanks to: Pauline Hallam (France), Sadie Weinbaum and the Federation for Underwater Activities in Israel, AquaSport and the Mediterranean and A. Dishon (Israel), Wade Doak and G. H. Patton (New Zealand), Paula Tebbs (Bermuda), Mike Warner (Kenya), Kelvin Moyses (Greece), Munci Giz (Turkey), F. Benmiloud (Algeria), Guy Webb (Baleric Islands), Sylvia Forde (Spain), and Dorothy Malcolm Smith (Australia).

My thanks to Cy Corder and Peter Scoones of Marine Unit for their help in picture research and for the illustrations which they provided; to Tony Timmington at Features International for his help with the photographs and to John Debley for the illustrations. Finally a word of thanks and appreciation to my admirable secratary, Jean Janes, for her work in typing a very difficult manuscript.

Contents

Photographs

1 The shackles of gravity cast aside, the skin-diver moves like a bird through the sunlit ocean   *facing page 16*

2 In cold, dark northern waters a diver wearing a full protective clothing works on the seabed. Here a special hydraulic gun is being used to drive steel spikes into the rocks during a survey (Photo: Cy Conden)   *facing page 16*

3 The basic equipment can be seen on this shot of a young diver at work in the Mediterranean. He is using a single hose demand valve. Exhaust bubbles stream away from beneath his mask. Note the pressure gauge hanging down to the left of the diver and the depth gauge on his wrist. In the warm waters of the south he can work without any protective clothing. Many divers prefer to keep their snorkel in the mask strap but this diver has his hanging from a line because of the risk it might get entangled with the cables he was working on   *facing page 17*

4 Divers kit up for a dive in the Channel. They are wearing full wet suits with hoods, both are diving with single hose demand valves. Note the quick release clip on the weight belt of the front diver. The rear diver is using a tadpole, a now obsolete type of tank which should be avoided second hand   *facing page 17*

5 The mask and snorkel in action. A self-portrait using an ultra wide angle lens during a snorkel dive off Cyprus. Note the full face mask. Water flooding down the snorkel tube is held in the mouth and blown clear on surfacing   *facing page 32*

6 An instructor from Number One Branch of the BSAC demonstrates correct mask fitting procedure. The mask is held in the left hand and all stray hair removed from the forehead   *facing page 32*

7 The straps are drawn back over the head   *facing page 33*

8 Mask clearing technique being practiced in a pool during a BSAC training session. Note the way the mask is held in place while exhaled air blows the water clear   *facing page 33*

All photographs by the author, except where stated.

Illustrations

Back to the Sea

We came from the sea before the dawn of history. Today we are going back to the sea, clad in neoprene, breathing compressed air, finning down to discover the secrets of this strange and silent world.

In this book I want to introduce skin-diving to readers who may be interested in the sport but not know exactly how to make a start. I describe the equipment required and how you should set about buying it both new and secondhand. I outline the physiological hazards and explain training procedures. But this is not a text-book which will train you to become a competent and safe diver, no book can do that, any more than you can read about driving a car and immediately become proficient behind the wheel. Diving is a skill which must be taught by a qualified instructor under carefully controlled conditions. At first probably in a pool and only then in shallow open water and deep sea. This book will provide sufficient theoretical groundwork to enable you to understand each stage of training and to appreciate the need for precautions which will be taught.

On the other hand I have tried to avoid making the early part of the book over complicated, because I think the general reaction to very complex sections is either to be put off the whole subject or to skip it! I believe that those limited areas of diving theory which strike many as complicated are best explained during training lectures when the beginner has a chance to ask questions and have them answered right away. Since this is not a diving manual, there are others far better qualified to write them for one thing, and anybody who takes up diving and becomes a member of the British Sub Aqua Club will receive what is probably the definitive diving text-book in any event, I have only dealt briefly with certain topics. The hazards of deep diving are discussed and mention is made of Decompression Tables, although I have deliberately not listed any examples of these tables. There could be a temptation for some self-taught divers to use them as a "passport" to deep diving without properly understanding the problems involved. Nor have I dealt with compressors, or decanting. Again I feel such information should be confined to diving manuals and backed up by lectures and supervised practical work.

The second part of the book is designed to help divers with some experience, perhaps one season's diving behind them, who feel quite at home underwater and are looking for subaqua pursuits to occupy their dives. Photography is dealt with at length for two main reasons. A

1

recent survey carried out by the British Sub Aqua Club found that photography is the number one underwater interest amongst the majority of divers. Furthermore, it is a fundamental tool of many other subaqua pursuits, from archaeology to marine biology. Finally perhaps I should declare a vested interest as my professional diving is on photographic assignments for newspapers and magazines.

Whole books have been written about each of the subjects dealt with in the second part of *Dive! Dive! Dive!* and I am well aware of the unavoidable condensation and omissions. For this reason I have included, at the end of every chapter, a list of further reading suggestions which will take enthusiasts as deeply into that particular specialisation as they want to go. I have avoided mentioning prices as far as possible as these change so often.

One underwater activity which is not covered is spear-fishing. This is partly because I am writing about air-diving and many countries, quite rightly, prohibit the taking of fish by such divers. One man using a hand spear, and his physical prowess to hunt in the depths may possibly still be termed a sportsman. But divers armed with powered spear guns who wear air cylinders on their backs deserve only the adjective butcher, as anybody who has dived in an area before and after it has been fished by aqualung divers must agree.

It is distaste for such slaughter and the state of mind it implies which is my main reason for not wishing to promote the cause of subaqua hunting in any way, a view which I am confident is shared by an increasing number of responsible divers. Recently the father of modern skindiving, Jacques Yves Cousteau resigned from the Presidency of the Confederation Mondiale des Activites Subaquatiques as a protest against the World Federation's stand on spear-fishing. "The sea is so vulnerable and helplessly endangered today . . ." he says. "I am not speaking just of the Mediterranean, I am speaking of everywhere. There is no place that has not been more or less devastated by divers . . . if there were ten spear-fishermen in the world it wouldn't matter much, but if you have ten million it is a disaster."

Much the same sentiments were echoed by science fiction writer Arthur C. Clarke when he told delegates to a world congress on diving, "We all know which is the most terrifying, most dangerous, most destructive creature in the sea; he's right here in the hall. The question which this generation has to answer is: can we exploit the sea without destroying it?"

The answer lies in the hands of all who use the sea for sport or profit. Unless the International Whaling Commission acts to save whales instead of the profits of Whaling Companies, our children will know about these fantastic creatures only at secondhand, from films and photographs. Unless skin-divers agree to stop taking trophies from wrecks and crayfish by the dozen then the more accessible seabed areas around our shores will soon become as lifeless and uninteresting as the deserts.

As divers, our attitude towards the sea is vitally important. Guy Gilpatrick, the American who pioneered free diving off the French coast in the 1920's, put on goggles and discovered a new world in the Mediterranean. A world without gravity where man becomes a bird in flight, a world of wrecks and awe-inspiring chasms, luxurious pastures and plunging cliffs, of a million species of life from the gigantic to the microscopic. Today that world is available to us all. The passports are specialised equipment, the knowledge of how to use it, and curiosity.

It is a beautiful world which man has only begun to explore in the last few decades. Our legacy to the divers of tomorrow must be an increase in the knowledge and understanding of the depths. Not the epitaph above wasteland of lifeless reefs and plundered wrecks "Mankind was Here".

Section One

Dive! Dive! Dive!

The contraband runner ran out of luck and sea on a night in late March, when the Mediterranean was lashed by a Force Nine gale. Her skipper, so the locals said, had been steaming without lights and hugging the shoreline to avoid detection by the Excise launches. It was a dangerous gamble and the skipper lost it. His vessel, an elderly cargo boat of some 600 tons, struck rocks reaching from deep water to within ten feet of the surface.

Months later, as I explored the wreck, I tried to picuture the events of that night in my mind. Finning through still water above the steeply angled decks, or plunging head-first down companion-ways, where only bright, darting fish disturbed the brooding peace of the vessel, it was hard to imagine the confusion that must have followed the disaster. With the Mediterranean whipped into a cauldron of fury, and no moon, the blackness of the storm would have been relieved only by spilling yellow cabin lights as hatches were flung open. The men had probably been asleep, snatched from the warmth of bunks onto decks slippery with sea and lashed by icy cold spray. Orders would have been lost in the screaming wind, men dazed by their abrupt transition from security to imminent danger.

But somehow the lifeboats were lowered and the crew all escaped. Only the cat was abandoned and crawled away into the comforting warmth of the galley to perish with the ship. Within a few minutes it was probably all over, but the old craft must have taken leave of this world to the accompaniment of a brutal cacophony of splintering timbers and collapsing bulkheads. A death march of destruction whose climactic finale was the bursting of her boiler.

Six months later, on a hot afternoon in September, a brightly painted wooden fishing boat, powered by a spluttering outboard, crawls like an inquisitive water beetle across the blue pancake of the Mediterranean. The nearest land, seen through the mid-morning heat haze, is no more than a featureless, blue-grey undulation on the horizon, as we near the wreck site.

Apart from myself there are three other skin-divers and an elderly fisherman aboard. He sits hunched over his helm, protected from the blazing sun by a large straw hat, chewing a slice of freshly cut melon. The trip had been arranged during lengthy but agreeable negotiations in a harbour bar, the previous evening. Of course he knew the wreck we meant, he had assured us. He could find it in a fog, blindfold!

We believed him and didn't ask too many questions. It was common knowledge that a great deal of illegal salvage had taken place on the site. In fact, probably no sooner had that fatal storm died away than the first local skin-divers were on the spot to lift anything that could be lifted, hammered, cut or prised loose. By now her carcass was undoubtedly picked clean. Not that we could have cared less, our object was exploration and photography, not loot.

"She's in good shape," the old fisherman had promised. "Not too much bust up." We hoped he was right. There are few more exciting things on which to dive than a really wreck like wreck.

The fisherman wipes juice from his stubbled chin with the back of a greasy left hand and kills the motor, by the simple expedient of shorting the plug with a piece of bent wire. The anchor is heaved over the side and we can watch the rope slither right to the seabed. With the sun almost vertical in the sky and the sea flat calm it is possible to make out the shape of the wreck as well. We kit up carefully in the cramped space. Although the water is warm at the surface a prolonged stay at sixty feet will be chilly so we are all wearing wet-suit jackets. The air cylinders are checked and harnesses adjusted, life-jackets and then weight belts put on. After spitting into my face mask I rinse it out in the sea to prevent misting. We are ready to go, backwards into the water falling two at a time from opposite sides of the frail boat, to prevent her from upsetting.

In the sea I have the usual moments of somersaulting confusion. Then I reorientate myself, check that everything is OK and surface again, following the silver saucers of exhaled air back into the sunlight.

I usually find my first moments in the sea amazingly exciting. The shackles of gravity have been cast aside. I am free to turn and twist at will, to soar and plunge like a bird. It's an excitement that can produce a childlike response, and I chase my air bubbles to the surface, slapping at the wobbling discs so that they shatter into a dozen smaller, gleaming saucers.

On the surface we pair up, signal that everything is OK and then turn back into the depths, following the magnified arc of anchor rope downwards with smooth, easy fin strokes. Sea speeds up sound, distorting it strangely, your breathing seems absurdly loud at first, the clink of metal on metal reverberates. On this dive visibility is excellent, sixty feet or more, reduced only by a fine haze of suspended matter. As we go deeper the colours change, red light is filtered out of the spectrum making bare hands ghostly white. If you cut yourself underwater at depth you bleed black blood!

In a few minutes we are close to the wreck and make a preliminary survey. The vessel is resting with her aft superstructure canted over to port. Forward of the bridge she is badly broken up and the deck falls steeply towards a gaping chasm which was once her forward cargo hold. A large winch has toppled onto the confusion of jagged metal, twisted cables and angled steel plates. The mast has come down and lies

8

a little distance from the wreck, attached only by trailing cables, already partly camouflaged by settling sand and weed.

The bow is still lined up with the stern, although now linked to it only by a narrow backbone of steel and the shambles of broken plates. The foremast thrusts boldly towards the surface like an accusing finger. I fin over and upwards. A topmost lamp remains in place. Above me, twenty-five feet away, the surface is a silvery blue expanse with a single black dot on it, the underside of our boat.

My diving partner heads down again towards the aft superstructure and I follow him, not too closely in case his fins knock my mask out of place. He flattens out over the sea bed and then pushes himself easily upwards, following the angle of the hull until he can flip gently over the aft rails. Before us is a deck cabin with an open doorway. He goes hesitantly inside and I follow into the gloom. After the brilliant sea it takes a few moments to adopt to the darkness. Then I can make out steel-framed bunks bolted along one side. The floor is covered with mounds of unidentifiable debris coated in sediment. My partner runs his hands through it making the sinister dimness even more obscure as clouds of dense silt mushroom upwards.

Then from the drifting fog a hand appears, pushing a triumphantly waggled trophy under my mask. It's an aluminium mug. Strange to think that the last hand to hold it belonged to a seaman who was bracing himself against the furious motion of this boat.

We leave the crew's quarters and enter the galley, a tiny slit of a room with an entrance on the port side of the vessel. The cooking range is still there, few pots and pans hanging above it. Cupboard doors hang open, their contents looted months before. Under the range my probing fingers close on a grim trophy, a skeleton! Not human, but feline. A cat's skull comes gleaming from the dark recess in which the unfortunate animal died. I replace it.

On the bridge, where the last fatal orders were given, the wheel is still in place but the instruments and all the brass have been removed. The propeller, a valuable item of salvage, has been left, we find. Perhaps the skills required to blow it off were beyond local skin-divers, or else it seemed too difficult to bring ashore illegally. Still I don't give much for that propeller's chances in the months to come. Our air supply is now low. We reluctantly leave the wreck and fin back to the surface. Boarding the diving boat is a delicate operation and the old fisherman watches the process anxiously clutching his tiller and drawing at a hand-rolled cigarette that seems to be mostly paper. When we, and all the equipment, have come aboard safely and his boat is still afloat he gives a toothless grin of relief and slices us each a large piece of melon as a reward for managing not to drown him.

Another month and a very different sea. The English channel, bottle green and choppy. A fine, cold November afternoon three miles off the South Coast of England. A larger boat this time and a bigger diving party, eight of us going to investigate the sea bed sixty feet below. The trawler, hired for this expedition, offers the luxury of a cabin in which to change into full wet-suits with hood, bootees and gloves to combat the cold northern waters. A local fisherman owns the boat, and often takes out divers. He confirms that we have ten minutes left before slack water. Not always the best time to dive, one of the worst times if you are looking for fish to photograph, this short period when the tide is on the turn does offer the safest and least exhausting conditions.

With the anchor let go and engine stopped the boat rises and falls briskly on the small waves. One or two of the divers are feeling a bit unhappy about conditions so the sooner we get below the surface the better. A blue and white flag is raised. It is the International Code of signals letter "A" which indicates "I have a diver down; keep well clear at slow speed."

As always equipment is checked carefully. Air supply, the quick release on harness and weight belt in case they have to be jettisoned in an emergency. Now it's time to go over the side. After a sudden shock as cold water floods into my wet suit, comes relief as the sea warms up in contact with my skin—aided perhaps by a tried and tested method.

I fin over to my companion. He makes a circle with thumb and first finger to show that all is well; then down we go. I am leading, following the anchor chain. The visibility is no more than two feet. The chain emerges and vanishes as abruptly in drifting clouds of tiny weed and suspended particles, the light bright despite the lack of clarity. We pass suddenly into a strata of dense dark water and visibility drops to less than ten inches as my depth gauge indicates forty feet. The light is dim now and the amount of suspended matter is still increasing. But suddenly, at fifty feet, we are through the worst and the sea becomes clear by comparison, although the level of light is low. It is as though I have flown through low cloud to emerge into clear air just above the ground. With a depth of fifty-five feet indicated on my gauge I abruptly see the bottom. One moment there is a swirling green-grey fog which parts like a sluggish curtain on my approach. Then, from the insubstantial matter, emerges solid shape. So unexpectedly does it appear that, for a moment, I am certain my mind is playing tricks. But no, the rocks are real enough as a tentative exploration with one gloved hand confirms. The ship's anchor has wedged in a crevice about two feet from me. Visibility has stabilised at three feet.

The red part of the spectrum is absorbed by the water, blue and violet light filtered out by dissolved vegetable matter, which is why, enhanced by plant plankton at certain times of the year, northern waters appear green. It is a rather drab world of dim light and low contrasts, of grey shapes which come and go like phantoms in a fog. A frightening world at first, in which it is all too easy to become confused, disorientated and lost. Using the anchor as a starting point I take a compass bearing and then fin off in a north-easterly direction. To make my return to the anchor will merely be a matter of back-tracking along the same bearing. That's the theory at any rate!

The seascape below is jagged rock covered with fine, sediment filmed weed which sways with the current. The floor rises slightly, and the depth gauge is registering forty-five feet when, suddenly, I am surrounded by well over a hundred dark, fearless fish. As my finning disturbs the sand and vegetation coating the rocks, they dart about, snatching at food and coming within inches of me. They are Bib, dark brown when mature, dark with lighter bands when young. The frequent and impudent companions of divers off northern coasts. They can be very bold. Some divers, trying to take pictures of them, have found the fish goggling curiously right into the lens window, undismayed even by gentle, discouraging smacks. They grow two feet in length, and have trailing sense organs called barbels (it means "small beard") beneath their mouths.

The rock formations are getting more crenellated and interesting. There are deep crevices and jagged depressions fringed with weed, red and brown algae, the ideal hiding place for more retiring species.

I feel an urgent tap on the shoulder. My companion is pointing towards a huge, dark, powerful monster of a fish cropping at the weed. As we swim cautiously towards this fish, he chews on unperturbed. Pieces of chewed weed drift from the large mouth of this magnificent cod as he feeds. One moment he is there, apparently unalarmed and tolerant of our presence, the next he has gone, flicking effortlessly off into the gloom.

This dive has one more adventure in store. In a flat depression between spurs of rock we come across a man-made object, the boiler of a long forgotten wreck probably. Its outline is too clearly curved to be natural, but marine crustaceans and weed have camouflaged it so well that a positive identification is impossible. It is not the wreckage itself that provides the focus of our interest, but a creature whose bullet-like head protrudes from the black depths of his secure lair, gold-rimmed eyes watching our approach. The head emerges further, jack-in-the-box like to snap at some passing tit-bit, invisible to us. This is the conger whose slate-coloured body is powerful and snake-like. They are said to be savage, but divers generally find them harmless, although they can be enormous. One weighing more than 250 lbs was trawled up off the coast of Iceland.

My companion removes his diving knife and offers the blade to the conger, who seems to eye it distainfully before retreating into his home. Perhaps he's been fooled that way once before.

With the air gauges registering enough to get back in safety, we head for the anchor chain on the compass bearing and miss it completely. So much for my navigation! However, it isn't that serious as we come up within twenty feet of the diving boat. Other heads are breaking the surface too. We signal that everything is OK and fin back to the trawler.

Another dive completed, more experience gained and cups of hot coffee to celebrate.

Two very different dives, unremarkable and yet like every dive, memorable in some way. Looking at the pictures afterwards, or just thumbing through the pages of a diving log brings it all to life again.

I have tried to give something of the flavour and excitement of the dives, but any description must at best be a pale imitation of reality, for every dive is a very personal experience. Perhaps it is the opportunity to become an individual again, in a society which grows increasingly bureaucratic and regimented, that attracts many to the sport. As a diver you have the responsibility of keeping an eye out for your diving companion, yet at the same time the pleasures you gain and ultimately your own safety, are a completely personal matter. The challenge to one's mental and physical resources are all too real and this too may form part of the attraction.

But it is more than just a question of losing or finding oneself in the depths. There can be a tremendous intellectual satisfaction in uncovering the secrets of the sea, for such is our present ignorance of an environment which occupies some 70% of this planet, even the amateur diver can play a very real part in advancing man's knowledge. Indeed the divers' situation is unique. Only he can carry out observations *in situ*. Only he can study and record the behaviour of fish in their natural habitat, observe the ecology of the seabed, sketch the exact lie of an ancient wreck or the foundations of a drowned city. Without his skill and courage, scientists could only grapple for their knowledge, like cloud borne giants dredging up scraps of information from the surface of the earth and trying to piece together our civilisation from the damaged fragments obtained.

A Start in Diving

The man who thinks he can learn skin-diving from a book, like the man who dives alone, is in a suicide club of one. Beneath the sea, as on it, safety depends on the equipment you use and the way you have been taught to use it. These skills, plus the confidence and self-discipline which enable you to think straight and act effectively in an emergency, can only be acquired during practical training sessions under qualified instructors. The course you follow must be carefully graded to take a beginner safely from the pool to open water diving. Not only will your survival depend on this training, so will your diving pleasure.

Diving is probably the world's fastest growing sport. Yet many men and women who feel they might be interested in taking it up are put off by the cost, because they feel great athletic prowess is demanded or simply because they don't know how to take the plunge.

Diving *is* fairly expensive, although there are perfectly safe ways of cutting the costs which I will describe in the next chapter. It is not, as one disillusioned yachtsman remarked of his hobby, as enjoyable and costly as tearing up five pound notes under a cold shower!

What about fitness? You have to be in reasonably good condition and healthy to dive safely. Fins may turn a poor swimmer into a fairly adequate one, but they can come off accidently and the diver who cannot make any effective progress through the sea without them could be in serious trouble. The British Sub Aqua Club has worked out a basic swimming test designed to check the stamina and ability in the water of prospective members. Potential Olympic champions are not being sought, just reasonable swimmers who could look after themselves in open water. The test is as follows:

1. Swim 200 metres using any front stroke.
2. Swim 100 metres using any back stroke.
3. Swim 50 metres wearing a weight belt. The weight is adjusted according to build, but is usually around 5 kg.
4. Float for five minutes.
5. Tread water for one minute with hands above head.
6. Dive six times to the bottom of the pool to retrieve an object.

Any properly organised club, whether or not it is a branch of the BSAC, should expect its members to undertake these tests. If they do not then you should regard them with grave suspicion. If you cannot do all these tests fairly comfortably then spend a few evenings at the pool building up confidence and stamina.

Diving is not just a man's sport, it is very much a sport for women too. Take, for instance, school teacher Margot Parker a housewife diver and a member of the Council of the British Sub Aqua Club. I first met Margot on an expedition in the West Country when we were helping to set up an underwater laboratory 30 feet below the surface of Plymouth Sound. It was tough work, humping iron ballast off a jetty and onto the base of the submerged steel laboratory. Margot was working beside Chez, her husband, who introduced her to the sport about seven years ago. During a coffee break on the windswept breakwater I asked her about the physical demands of diving on a woman. "It as much more to do with whether a person can adapt themselves to the environment. It's in the mind whether you are a good diver or a bad one," she told me.

And that just about sums it up! Supermen and Superwomen are not required, neither are inflated bank balances nor, above all, are dare-devils with James Bond complexes. A reasonable ability in the water, the sort of fitness that we all can, and should, attain in order to keep healthy, and a desire to dive. These are your passports to a new, exciting world of unlimited horizons. The silent domain of the sea.

2

Buying Your Equipment

The uninitiated, watching a group of black clad, flippered figures plodding in a clumsy line across a shingle strand at the start of a dive, may be forgiven for wondering why on earth the sport was ever called skindiving! Skin seems the last thing in evidence during a dive in bleak northern waters. Wearing neoprene wet-suits, hooded, masked and gloved, weighed down by cylinders, demand valve, lead belt, instruments, knife and perhaps clutching a camera in a cumbersome underwater case, the land bound skin-diver presents a comic, ungainly sort of image. To my mind the only good thing about a difficult entry from some isolated and pebble strewn beach, is the way it heightens that magic moment as the sea closes around you, gravity is conquered and the ugly duck diver finds transformation into a man-fish. Now the equipment, which weighed so heavily a few moments before, plays its part in keeping the diver safe, relaxed and confident, free to explore the world beneath the waves.

At least that's the sort of state your equipment should produce. Whether or not it does will depend on each piece being capable of doing the job for which it was designed, built and purchased. Capable through the competence and care of its construction, the treatment which is has received at the hands of those who use it and the way it is used. During a dive your safety depends on your equipment. If any of the basic items let you down, a potentially serious situation may develop. They say that at sea a man can survive bad luck or bad judgement but not a combination of both. Luck is, I believe, very much in our own hands to create; judgement must start long before any diving takes place, at the moment you buy your equipment. In this chapter I want to look at the various pieces of equipment you will need to buy, and discuss the sort of considerations which should be in the mind of a newcomer to the sport when he sets about building up his diving gear.

Because some of the items needed are expensive, many divers cut costs by purchasing second hand equipment, especially air cylinders and demand valves. There is nothing wrong with this provided certain safeguards are followed, especially when buying used air bottles. But never buy equipment about which you are even slightly unhappy just because it is cheap. Demand valves, for example, are very much a personal value judgement. Given that a range of designs are all perfectly reliable and well made, one diver will feel at home using one type, while another just can't get on with it at all. If he buys this valve secondhand because he can save a few pounds, his diving may be safe but less

2

enjoyable than it should be.

As I will explain in the next chapter, learning to relax and feel at home underwater may take several dives. The newcomer is naturally apprehensive about entering this new, strange and potentially dangerous environment. Sound training and a careful introduction to open water diving, under the guide of an experienced and skilled instructor, can eliminate many of these fears. However, a measure of anxiety is always likely to exist even amongst the best divers prior to every dive. I do not mean fear, but that sharpening of the senses which is part of man's basic survival kit. This ensures that all the necessary checks are made and each aspect of the proposed dive is considered in advance in order to iron out possible dangers.

It is foolish to add to this normal anxiety through uncertainty about your equipment. Do not try and save money at the cost of your confidence. Choose each item with care, ask other divers their opinion, go to a professional dealer—he will probably be an enthusiastic diver himself—and ask his advice. If you have trained, as I advised in the previous chapter, through a well organised club, then you will have had at least pool experience using their equipment. This should give you further guidance. If the club was using double-hose demand valves, did you find these comfortable, or too restrictive? Was the back-pack on the air-cylinder comfortable or did it feel awkward even when carefully adjusted to your measurements? Did you find the weight belt release clips quick and easy to manipulate?

Build up equipment experience before purchasing major items, do not rush out in the first burst of enthusiasm and spend hard earned money on the most chrome plated, brashly illustrated gear you can find. At all stages buy and treat diving equipment as though your life depended on it—it does!

Before you dive with an aqualung you will probably have done some snorkelling in open water, you will certainly have gone through a course of snorkel training if you are learning to dive through a club. This basic equipment, fins, face-mask and snorkel tube, costing a total of around £8, you will have to provide yourself on joining a club. Even where these simple items are concerned, care must be taken in their purchase and you should always go to a qualified dealer rather than pick them up at a seaside souvenir shop where brightly coloured masks—some of them potential killers—dangle between sticks of rock, saucy postcards and mermaids in glass globes.

The Diving Mask
In order to be able to see under the sea the diver must place an airspace between his eyes and the water. Because of *refraction* doing so makes underwater objects look a third larger, and therefore closer, than they actually are. This is a problem which I will discuss further in the next chapter and in the chapters on underwater photography. Although a fairly simple

and relatively inexpensive piece of equipment, the mask is probably the most important single item a diver owns. Without a regulator you can snorkel dive, if you lose your fins you can still manage to get along. But if the mask lets you down vision is lost and the sea around you becomes a blur in which only light and dark can be distinguished. This, together with such water as an inexperienced diver may inadvertently inhale, can easily produce the serious psychological state known as *diver panic* in which all the wrong decisions are liable to be made.

Choose your mask with care, when you pick from the very wide range of designs—there are more than 180 different types of mask —and prices on offer.

The first essential is that the mask fits well and feels comfortable. It should have a skirt, that part contoured to fit the face, which is soft and pliable. The area of skin between the nose and upper lip is tender, and if the mask is moulded from stiff rubber or has to be clamped tightly against the skin to prevent leaks because it is a poor fit, then the discomfort may be considerable.

To test the fit of a mask simply place it against your face, having first made certain you have not left any hair in the way, and inhale. A correctly fitting mask should remain pressed against the face without support from the straps. As you exhale it should drop off.

The front of the mask may be made either from perspex or safety glass. Perspex mists up more readily and is easier to scratch than glass which makes glass preferable provided it is toughened glass. Make certain that this word is printed on the material before bothering to waste any further time testing the mask. The face glass should be held in position by a metal clamp and this, like any other parts, must be made from a non-corrosive material. The retaining strap should be of the double or split type.

In order to dive it is necessary to "clear" the ears, exactly why will be explained in Chapter Three. In order to achieve clearing the diver must hold the nose. For this reason your mask should be moulded with a shaped nosepiece, known as a compensator.

How much vision you require is rather a matter of choice. Some masks will give you 90° vision which many divers find perfectly adequate, however it is possible to buy wrap around masks which allow 180° vision.

Underwater the weight of the mask is not of much consequence, but if you have to hang around in a boat or on the beach prior to diving with the mask in place then the heavier versions may cause discomfort. The range of weights available is quite considerable, from under six ounces to well over a pound. As when choosing a mask for vision the weight, provided that the fit is comfortable, is really a matter of preference.

Some types are fitted with a purge valve which enables you to clear water from the mask, and many divers find this a useful gadget. But it can be a source of leaks and, although it takes a moment longer, clearing

The shackles of gravity cast aside, the skin-diver moves like a bird through the sun light ocean. (See chapter one)

The mask and snorkel in action. A self-portrait of the author using an ultra wide angle lens during a snorkel dive off Cyprus. Note the full face mask. Water flooding down the snorkel tube is held in the mouth and blown clear on surfacing. (See chapter two)

The basic equipment can be seen on this shot of a young diver at work in the Mediterranean. He is using a single-hose demand valve. Exhaust bubbles stream away from beneath his mask. Note the pressure gauge hanging down to the left of the diver and the depth gauge on his wrist. In the warm waters of the south he can work without any protective clothing. Many divers prefer to keep their snorkel in the mask strap but this diver has his hanging from a line because of the risk it might get entangled with the cables he was working on. (See chapter two)

Divers kit up for a dive in the Channel. They are wearing full wet suits with hoods, both are diving with single hose demand valves. Note the quick release clip on the weight belt of the front diver. The rear diver is using a tadpole, a now obsolete type of tank which should be avoided second hand. (See chapter two)

water from an ordinary mask is really quite a simple matter which is part of the basic diver training programme.

If you wear glasses do not worry that you will have to make do without them underwater. Special frames can be bought to hold lenses inside the mask. A rather more expensive answer is to have the lenses ground into the glass of the mask itself.

Before leaving the subject of masks two warnings. Do not buy goggles and a nose clip, even for snorkelling. As you dive the increased pressure pushes the mask, or goggles against your face. With a mask you can equalise the pressure merely by exhaling through the nose. With goggles this is obviously impossible and a painful squeezing can result.

Under no circumstances should the combined mask and snorkel tube be bought. These are extremely dangerous pieces of equipment. For one thing carbon dioxide can build up in the face mask causing serious contamination, for another the ping-pong valves are dangerously inefficient and liable to flood.

The Snorkel—a short tube ending in a moulded mouthpiece

This is perhaps the simplest, cheapest piece of equipment you will need. But don't treat its purchase lightly because of that. In skin diving the snorkel-tube can be used, when the water is clear enough, for surveying the sea bed. More frequently the snorkel tube is used when swimming out from the shore to the diving area, or for swimming back to land or the diving boat at the end of a dive when your air supply is low.

When wearing diving equipment at the surface, the diver is forced to swim in a face downwards position and so the snorkel tube is an essential item. The tube should be no more than 14" (35 cm) long with an internal diameter of around half an inch (1.25 cm). It may be made of either plastic or aluminium. Many divers prefer the metal tubes, but if you use one watch out for others. You can cause a serious injury for example by surfacing suddenly under another diver. The mouthpiece, normally made from moulded rubber, is held lightly between the teeth. In use the snorkel is held in place by slipping it under the mask strap.

Snorkels which have a bent tube at the open end should be avoided as they can snag on underwater objects. Snorkels which have a ball valve even if not attached to masks, are not only useless but potentially dangerous. The valve can jam open or shut. In either event the result for the diver in unpleasant. It is also possible for the ping-pong ball used to collapse under pressure and jam in the tube.

Fins

As with the mask, so long as certain considerations are borne in mind, the choice of fins is a matter of personal preference. There are two basic types, those which slip on like a shoe and those which can be adjusted

17

with a strap. If you prefer the strap variety then it will pay to make regular checks of both strap and fastener as they are a potential source of weakness.

If you have not swum with fins before, I would advise against buying a very large, heavy pair as these can be extremely tiring to use. The fitting should be comfortable but not too loose as this may cause chaffing and blisters. One problem of fitting this type of fin occurs when swopping from wet-suit bootees, necessary for diving in northern waters in winter, to barefoot summer diving in warmer waters. A fin which is correct when using bootees will probably be too large when used without. The answer is either to buy two pairs, one for use with and one for use without bootees, or use the adjustable strap type. Incidentally, if a young boy or girl takes up snorkelling it is as well to buy the strap-type fin at first as this allows for growing feet.

Wet Suits

Whether you are snorkel or skin diving in northern water you will need some form of protection against the cold. Any type of garment which traps body warmed water against the skin is useful, an old pullover is better than nothing when snorkel diving, but for lengthy immersion it is essential to have a correctly designed protective clothing.

The costume worn by most sports divers is termed a "wet suit" because water enters between the body and the neoprene material, (neoprene is a form of rubber containing millions of small nitrogen bubbles) and the body quickly warms up the trapped water while the bubbles provide effective insulation against heat loss. It is, incidently, an insulation which becomes less efficient on deep dives as water pressure compresses the neoprene.

There is another type, the dry-suit, which protects the diver completely against the sea, by means of water-tight seals at the wrists, neck and ankles. Warmth is then provided by the diver wearing pullovers and woollen garments under the suit. For most amateur divers these more complicated and costly suits are unnecessary.

Wet suits can be bought off the peg, made to measure by diver supply firms or, least expensively of all, made up at home either from kits or using only the raw materials and a fair amount of do-it-yourself skill.

The fit of the finished suit must be snug, in order to combine satisfactory insulation with ease of movement. Neoprene is available in different weights, the most popular being between 5 mm and 8 mm.

A full wet suit consists of trousers, jacket, hood and bootees. All of them are essential protection in cold waters where hyperthermia, which I shall discuss in the next chapter, can be a real hazard. For ease of putting on, a lined suit—the lining is either nylon or jersey material—is advisable. Unlined neoprene has to be smothered in French chalk or the body lubricated with washing up liquid, before one can wriggle into it.

18

This is a point to watch out for if buying a secondhand wet suit through a newspaper or magazine advertisement.

After a sea dive, the suit, together with mask and fins, should be rinsed in fresh water before being put away.

Store the suit carefully—do not fold it—out of season, and give the material a light coating of talcum powder or French chalk to keep it supple. The zips should be lightly lubricated with silicone grease.

Weight belt

A neoprene wet suit makes the swimmer very positively buoyant. It becomes not merely difficult to sink but virtually impossible. To compensate for this and to overcome the body's own natural buoyancy, a weight belt must be worn.

The belt consists of a length of material, canvas or leather, with a quick release mechanism to enable a diver in difficulties to ditch the whole lot in a second. It is essential that this quick release mechanism is foolproof and large enough to be operated easily with cold numbed fingers. The weights themselves are made from lead and how much ballast will be needed to obtain the vitally necessary state of neutral buoyancy—in which the swimmer neither sinks nor rises—will vary from diver to diver. Some people are naturally very positively buoyant and need quite a lot of weight to make them neutral, others require much less.

These five items—mask, snorkel, fins, wet suit and weight belt, form the basic diving equipment needed for snorkelling and preliminary bath training for skin diving. Any worthwhile club will be able to provide the more expensive pieces of gear needed during instruction. In addition to these items you should give careful consideration to a life-jacket, even for snorkelling. For skin diving it is essential and most clubs will not allow you to go on an open water dive without one.

Lifejackets

These come in two types. There is the jacket intended for inflation, either by mouth or a small CO_2 bottle, only in an emergency. These are known as surface jackets and are acceptable for snorkelling and provide some degree of safety when skin diving. However, as you become accomplished you will certainly want to do more than just potter around underwater. Perhaps you will take up photography, archaeology, wreck hunting or marine biology. For all these tasks it may be very useful to have a means by which you can vary your buoyancy at will. For example, supposing you have adjusted your weights correctly for normal swimming. On the bottom you find an interesting trophy which, bearing in mind the cautions I shall outline in Chapters Seven and Eight, you decide to lift to the surface. Picking it up will make you more negatively buoyant and, if the object is large and heavy, you may find it very hard to return to the fresh air. If you have an adjustable buoyancy life jacket, usually referred to as a ABLJ, you can compensate by slightly inflating

19

the jacket—it works from a small bottle of compressed air—to make yourself more positively buoyant. These jackets are more expensive than the surface variety, between £30 and £50, and can be exceedingly dangerous in the wrong hands. If the jackets are inflated incautiously by inexperienced divers, they may shoot them surfacewards like a Polaris missile, inflicting serious physiological damage in the process. The correct use of an ABLJ is taught during a BSAC course.

Lifejackets must be treated with care, stored sensibly and checked regularly to make sure they inflate without leaking, the mouth tube hasn't perished and the emergency gas bottle still functions.

Now let us look at the more complicated and costly pieces of diving equipment, the demand valve and air cylinder. In the next chapter I shall discuss the effects of diving on the body and explain the physical laws which govern man's return to the sea. But in order to understand why a demand valve costs a fair amount of money and what you ought to expect from one, it is necessary to understand how they work.

The basic principle of the demand valve is extremely simple. It is designed to deliver air to the lungs at a pressure equal to the surrounding environment. At sea level we breath air at a pressure of 14.7 lbs per square inch. Because we are born under this pressure, caused by the weight of the atmosphere above our heads, the muscular development of our chests and diaphrams can normally cope with the task quite effortlessly.

When we dive we add the weight of water above us to the weight of air, or atmospheric pressure. At a depth of 33 feet the weight of water is equal to the weight of the atmosphere at the surface. The combined pressures now acting on our body, against which the respiratory muscles have to work, is therefore doubled. In fact, the body is quite incapable of working unaided at this depth, or indeed any depth below about two feet. The only way a diver can breathe is if the air entering his body, via his cylinder and demand valve, is delivered at a pressure equal to the surrounding water. This is why divers can not breathe by simply poking a long tube up to the surface. Instead of being able to draw air down the tube it is much more likely that water pressure would force the contents of the divers lung up it—an unattractive prospect!

The demand valve provides air at exactly the right pressure by means of a system which can be described simply as a metal box divided in two by a rubber membrane. Water is allowed into the box on one side of the membrane, high pressure air from the cylinder into the other side of the box. Attached to the membrane is a lever which controls the escape of air from the cylinder. A tube leading to the diver's mouthpiece leads from this compartment.

When the diver takes a breath, air is sucked out from the box. The membrane, under pressure from the water, is pushed inwards and the lever opens the valve to the air cylinder allowing high pressure air to flow into the box. This has the effect of pushing back the membrane until the pressure of the air and the pressure of the water are equalised. At this point the lever returns to a neutral position and shuts off the supply of air from the cylinder. Every time the diver takes a breath this process is repeated.

Because the pressure of air must always equalise the pressure of water, the diver receives this air at exactly the right pressure. If he dives deeper the membrane requires more air to return it to a neutral position, than in shallower waters.

In practice the design of demand valves has to be considerably more complicated than this rather basic explanation might suggest. Furthermore, because they operate under high pressure and must stand up to tough treatment generally, the manufacture of demand valves has to be of a very high standard. Precision engineering, expensive materials and careful checking at every stage of construction all help to push up the price.

Demand Valves
These attract more diver loyalty than any other piece of equipment. One man will swear by twin-hose valves, another only use the single hose type. As I said earlier, you should ask for advice, listen to the experiences of other divers using different designs of valves, and also gain as much experience using both the single and twin hose types before finally making up your mind.

The twin-hose, as its name implies, has two tubes which pass over the diver's shoulders to meet at a central mouthpiece. The demand valve is mounted above the cylinder behind the diver's head.

The single-hose separates the two stages of the valve which, in the twin-hose are both housed in the one container. The first stage, mounted above the bottle, reduces the air pressure to around 100 lbs per square inch. This air is then passed along a medium pressure tube to a second stage valve fitted to the diver's mouthpiece.

The twin-hose has large tubes which, when flooded with water, may require quite an effort to blow them clear. On the other hand, they have the advantage of removing exhaled air away from the diver's face. One tube delivers air, the other removes used air. With a single-hose valve used air bubbles streaming up before the mask can obscure vision and make photography rather more difficult. It is possible, however, to fit small deflectors which divert the flow of stale air away from the face.

The second disadvantage of the single-hose is that the extra weight on the mouthpiece can make them tiring to use for an extended period. Manufacturers overcome this by fitting straps which can be fastened around the neck to help support the mouthpiece and second stage. This is a good idea but for safety the fastening should be such that the mouthpiece can be easily and quickly removed in an emergency. A more recent idea, which probably helps to take some of the fatigue out of holding a heavy regulator, is a mouthpiece which moulds itself to the diver's own teeth and spreads a load normally borne by between four and eight teeth over twelve to sixteen. Although I have never dived with this piece of equipment, I have received good reports from a few divers who have, and it is said to be particularly comfortable for those who wear dental plates. The mouth piece, made by Farallon, has a plastic material on the lugs. Before use the diver holds the mouthpiece under a hot tap and then bites firmly, moulding the softened plastic into exactly the right shape of his mouth.

Demand valves, whatever their type, are attached to an air cylinder by means of a screw adjustor and an "O" ring seal.

These "O" rings may be made of polythene or neoprene rubber. Both are satisfactory although neoprene will probably last longer. You should always carry some spare "O" rings in your diving bag, they cost only a few pence but if they blow and you don't have a spare then diving will be impossible.

Air Cylinders (Bottles)

Perhaps because they look tough and rather uninteresting bottles often get treated with scant respect. However, an air cylinder which has been roughly handled and poorly stored may be unsafe to use and make a dangerous secondhand buy. Because cylinders, perhaps more than any other equipment, are bought secondhand, I shall discuss the precautions you need to take to avoid getting landed with a rogue bottle at some length.

Cylinders are made from either steel or aluminium. Despite the extra cost aluminium bottles are becoming increasingly popular because they are light and impervious to a major form of corrosion.

A cylinder should be neutrally or positively buoyant. A few steel cylinders are so negatively buoyant that they will sink a diver without a weight belt being necessary. This is extremely dangerous without an adjustable buoyancy life jacket, as the diver may have great difficulty surfacing in an emergency. My advice is to avoid these bottles if you are offered them secondhand.

Cylinders have different capacities and working pressures. It is hard to judge the capacity of a particular bottle from external dimensions or to judge which of two cylinders has the greater capacity, because one may have a far higher working pressure than the other. The capacity, expressed usually as cubic feet, is the volume of air which is needed to bring the cylinder up to its working pressure.

The Home Office has laid down specifications for the manufacture of cylinders used in the UK and these must be die-stamped onto the side of the bottle, together with the following information. (1) Serial number. (2) Manufacturer's test mark. (3) Rated charging pressure. (4) Test pressure. Bottles are normally tested at about $1\frac{1}{2}$ times their normal working pressure. Bottles also have to be checked again at the end of three years and then at intervals of two years for the rest of their working lives. A test certificate will be issued and no secondhand bottle should be purchased unless a current certificate can be produced. But even an in date certificate is no guarantee that the bottle is one hundred per cent sound. Not long ago such a bottle was being filled when it was noticed that air was escaping. When the cylinder was cut open heavy corrosion was found.

When buying a secondhand cylinder, having first checked the certificate and made sure the serial number on the form and that stamped on the bottle coincide, carry out a visual assessment. Does the bottle look like its been knocked around? Is the pillar valve battered and chipped? Has it very recently been repainted, a move possibly designed to cover up something rather nasty underneath?

Now check the specifications stamped on the side. In February, 1974 *Diver* magazine reported that rogue tanks were being illegally constructed from old CO_2 cylinders designed for use by brewers and publicans. These are dangerous for two reasons. First their working pressure of 1930 p.s.i. is lower than the normal working pressure of diving cylinders (2000/2250 p.s.i). This means such bottles might get regularly over charged leading to a possible explosion. Secondly, during the course of "conversion" part of the bottle may have been machined away leaving the metal dangerously thin. Any heat treatment on the bottle during the conversion will also have weakened the metal. To avoid being taken in you should examine the die stamped information carefully. At the very end of the specifications these tanks will be marked CO_2. Avoid them.

Avoid also a small tank, very widely available a few years ago, known as a "tadpole". This was a steel cylinder originally designed, I believe, for supplying compressed air to aircraft braking systems. They were steel and even if they are offered with a test certificate should be avoided because at the time I write it is impossible to tell what degree of internal corrosion may afflict them.

Once you have ensured that the cylinder really was designed and built for use by divers, open the tap and turn the bottle upside down. Shake it energetically. If any drops of water appear from a steel cylinder it could indicate serious internal corrosion. Avoid it.

Aluminium cylinders cannot rust, but they can be corroded by pitting caused by water and accelerated by high pressure oxygen in the air.

Even if insufficient water is present inside a cylinder to trickle out when shaken—there is an anti-rust tube inside the bottles which prevents all the liquid coming out—there may still be sufficient inside to have caused corrosion. Listen to the bottle, if it makes a rustling or swishing noise when shaken this could spell trouble.

Having bought a cylinder, new or secondhand, look after it. Wash it under fresh water after each dive, taking particular care to rinse around the harness band which can be a salt trap.

Paint the bottle occasionally. When not in use store upright, so that any water collects at the base where the stresses are lower and corrosion less serious. If you intend to leave the cylinder unused for some time then reduce the pressure of air inside to avoid the corrosion accelerating effect of the oxygen under pressure. If a cylinder is to remain unused for a really lengthy period it is worthwhile to have the pillar valve removed. The bottle can then be checked for corrosion and remedial action taken where necessary. Replace the valve and have the bottle charged at around 10 ats for storage. This positive pressure prevents moisture entering the cylinder.

Pressure Gauge

It is essential to know how much air you have left in your bottle and the most straight-forward method is to have a gauge which is fitted by pressure hose to the high pressure stage of the demand valve or the cylinder manifold. Some divers dislike using a gauge, fearing that its hose may get caught up when they are exploring a wreck. However, the risk is very slight and more than compensated by the ability to keep a constant check on the air supply.

Some demand valves are fitted with a restricting device which makes breathing harder as the air supply becomes low, thus forcing the diver to surface. Other tanks have a reserve supply which can be operated by pulling down a lever. This reserve is sufficient for the diver to surface from all but the deepest dives safely.

Harness and back-pack

There are a number of different designs on the market, and final selection can be based on personal preferences. If using aluminium cylinders take advice from your dealer as some metals used in the bottle clamps can cause corrosion due to electrolytic action. The webbing harness should be fitted with easily operated quick release catches in case you need to jettison the whole lot in an emergency.

Knife

This should be made from stainless steel with a strong blade, preferably with a cutting and a saw edge. The handle should be solid enough to use as a hammer, the blade solid down to the point so that it won't snap off when being used as a crowbar, screwdriver, gouge or any of the other multiplicity of uses found for it underwater. The knife should be kept in a sheath which is normally fastened to the leg. Care must be taken when using a knife underwater because the sea softens the skin and makes a wound less painful. It is easy to hurt yourself quite badly and only realise the extent of the damage on surfacing.

Depth Gauge

There are various designs on the market which may work on slightly different principles. Go for accuracy rather than cheapness if you intend to make deep dives, and choose one with large numerals so that it can be easily read even in poor visibility.

Watch

Essential for deep diving where it may be necessary to make decompression stops on the way back. A rotating bezel which enables elapsed time to be read directly is valuable. As with a depth gauge the numerals should be easy to read in poor light.

Compass

Getting lost underwater often requires very little effort! A good compass will set you swimming in the right direction, not around in bewildered circles. It can be worn strapped to the wrist or on a lanyard and should be robust enough to take inevitable knocks when you are clambering in and out of a diving boat. When in use make sure it isn't being affected by any ferrous metal equipment such as a diving knife.

These then are the basic items in a skin-divers kit-bag. Choose each carefully, buy only after considering alternative designs available, and look after every item with care. Although the initial outlay for this sport is fairly heavy, such equipment is well made and designed to last for many years.

During training you will be taught how to use every item safely and efficiently. But there is one other piece of equipment that must be fully understood before safe diving can begin. Your own body!

3

The Body in the Water!

In skin-diving as in other such potentially hazardous sports as sailing, mountaineering or pot-holing, safety depends on a combination of reliable equipment which has been properly maintained and used, and a careful training in all aspects of the sport.

In the previous chapter we looked at equipment and in the next I shall be outlining the type of training programme which takes newcomers safely and smoothly from the pool to the open sea. Before dealing with training, however, we must pause to examine the effect of diving on the one piece of equipment that comes free of charge—the body.

Unlike the other action sports which I mentioned, skin-diving subjects the body to unique physiological stresses, largely as a result of having to breath air under pressure. These problems must be understood before any serious diving starts in order to identify and eliminate the risks. It is also necessary to appreciate the special psychological strains of diving so that they too can be overcome. As the Parachute Brigade boys say—"knowledge conquers fear."

Most people will be familiar with the basic functions of the respiratory and circulatory systems of the human body. However, for the sake of clarity in the discussion that follows it may be helpful to sketch in the broad outlines of the systems here.

Breathing is normally an automatic process geared to the demands of the body. At rest we breath quietly, sitting reading this chapter you will be breathing between ten and sixteen times a minute. Under exertion the body cells demand more oxygen and we begin to draw air at a greater rate.

In order to breath, the chest muscles raise the ribs upwards and outwards, whilst the diaphram—a broad sheet of muscle which forms the lower side of the chest cavity—is pulled downwards. The lungs now expand, to fill the partial vacuum, as air is drawn into them via the windpipe (Trachea) and the nose or throat. To exhale, the rib cage is lowered and the diaphram relaxes reducing the capacity of the chest and forcing air outwards. As I explained in the last chapter we breath air at sea level under atmospheric pressure of 14.7 lbs per square inch.

Under atmospheric pressure there are no problems about taking in oxygen and expelling poisonous carbon dioxide, the waste product produced by body cells. This exchange takes place inside the lungs, whose area is tremendously increased by thousands of air sacs (alveoli) which, when seen under a microscope, resemble bunches of grapes on stalks. It is through the thin walls of the alveoli that the exchange of

26

gases takes place. The red corpuscles in the blood stream discharge carbon dioxide and take up oxygen which is then circulated to the body tissue.

The blood supply, maintained by the heart, circulates through a network of arteries, veins and very fine capillaries. Oxygen-rich blood from the lungs flows into the left side of the heart and is pumped through arteries to all parts of the body. The oxygen is taken up by the cells and replaced by carbon dioxide and other waste products. The blood then passes through large and small veins to the right side of the heart and from there into the lungs to start the cycle all over again. To maintain this flow, the heart, in a relaxed state, will contract about 70 times per minute. At certain points on the body, for example behind the ear and on the underside of the wrist, where arteries pass over bones, these rythmic contractions can be felt as a "pulse."

The air we breath consists of a mixture of gases. About 78% is an inert gas, nitrogen. Oxygen forms 21%, and carbon dioxide about 0.03%. The difference is made up by five inert gases (argon, helium, crypton, neon and xeon) which need not concern us here although one of them, helium, does have a role to play in conquering the depths of the oceans.

Under normal atmospheric pressure nitrogen, which plays no part in the vital exchange of gases, merely dissolves into the blood fluid (plasma) which carries the red corpuscles around the body and then dissolves out again. No chemical reaction takes place.

Decompression Sickness

What happens when we add the pressure of water to the atmospheric pressure? At a depth of 33 feet the weight of water as we have seen becomes equal to the normal weight of air at sea level. This means that the body is under a combined pressure of air and sea. This total is termed *absolute pressure.*

Most of our body consists of solid matter and liquids which cannot be compressed to any serious extent by this increase in pressure, but the chest cavity is very vulnerable and would be crushed by the weight of water pressing in on it at any great depth. More important, as I explained in the previous chapter, the muscles of the chest are just not capable of exerting themselves against more than a very slight increase in external pressure.

The aqualung with its cylinder of compressed air and demand valve, overcomes this problem by delivering air at a pressure equal to that of the surrounding environment. Because of this, so far as the respiratory mechanism is concerned the diver has no problem. However, the way the gases are absorbed into the blood stream, and the effects they have on the brain under pressure are different and present a serious difficulty.

Nitrogen normally dissolves in and out of the blood plasma without any difficulty, but if you dive below a hundred feet, or stay at a shallower depth for an extended period, a great deal of nitrogen under pressure is dissolved into the body tissues. If the diver suddenly surfaces, reducing the pressure abrubtly, not all this dissolved nitrogen has time to pass out of the body in the normal way. The most frequently quoted analogy to describe what happens, is to liken the situation to suddenly opening a bottle of fizzy drink. As the pressure is released, carbon dioxide in the liquid forms bubbles. The same thing can happen to the nitrogen dissolved in the body tissues. Bubbling produces a variety of symptoms, from the painful to the extremely serious. These are termed decompression sickness.

If nitrogen forms bubbles in the cartilage of the knee or shoulder joint, it results in a pain which can vary from a dull ache, sometimes confused by divers with normal weariness following a dive, to the most excruciating agony. These are called the "bends", they cause a diver to bend double in pain and can strike between twenty and sixty minutes after a dive, or they may not be felt for some hours. The only answer is for the victim to be recompressed to allow the nitrogen to dissolve back into the blood out of the body.

A far more serious form of decompression sickness, and fortunately a rare one, is called the *chokes* from the tight constriction felt across the chest. This is caused by a large number of bubbles forming and interfering with the breathing circulation. Recompression is essential and it will almost certainly to necessary to rush a sufferer to a land based recompression chamber, a large, boiler like structure in which changes of pressure can be achieved mechanically. The victim is locked into the chamber, often with a doctor, and then rapidly put under a pressure equal to a deep dive.

But do not now throw up your hands in horror and decide to take up stamp collecting instead of skin-diving. Decompression sickness is the grim result of disregarding, either through ignorance or stupidity clearly defined diving procedures. A trained diver who keeps to the rule book should never encounter any difficulties.

Air Embolism

The relationship between pressure and volume is governed by a remarkably simple physical law (Boyles Law) which states that as you double the pressure you halve the volume. Take a bucket and turn it upside down. On the surface it will be filled with air, carry the bucket down to 33 feet (one atmosphere of extra pressure) and the air will be compressed so that it now fills half the bucket. However, to halve that volume again you must descend not another 33 feet (making three atmospheres absolute) but to 99 feet (four atmospheres absolute).

The importance of Boyles Law to the diver, is the way it decreases the air supply the deeper you descend. For example a 60 cubic foot bottle on the surface will last a normal person, breathing quietly and not over exerting himself, about sixty minutes. But if that same bottle is taken down to 33 feet its volume will be effectively halved and it will now last only 30

28

minutes. However to reduce the volume by half again, giving fifteen minutes of air, you would need to descend to 99 feet.

If you take a lungful of air at 100 feet and holding your breath, head for the surface, that air will expand. Your lungs are fairly elastic but there is a limit to what they can take and the rapid increase in volume is certain to rupture the fine membranes, causing bubbles of air to form in the blood. This is serious and possibly fatal. It should be emphasised that air embolism can occur at relatively shallow depths and you can be at risk even in a swimming pool which has a depth of more than fifteen feet. The answer is always to exhale on the way up, and under no circumstances, hold a breath of cylinder air during an ascent.

Nitrogen Narcosis—Oxygen Narcosis
Breathing air under pressure can cause two other problems during deep dives. The most common is nitrogen poisoning or narcosis. Large quantities of this gas dissolving into the blood stream have a strange effect on the brain. Divers begin to hallucinate. They may become convinced they can breath water and tear out their breathing tubes. The remedy is a prompt return to shallower water. Nitrogen narcosis, poetically dubbed 'rapture of the deep," by Jacques Cousteau, tends to creep up on the diver and affects people at different speeds. During a deep dive you should always keep an eye on your diving companion and be alert for any abnormal behaviour which may be caused by narcosis

Oxygen, life supporting under normal pressures, can become a poison at great depths. However this is unlikely to become a hazard during normal sports diving expeditions.

Ear Clearing
As you dive pressure builds up on the ear drum, a sensitive membrane which lies at the end of the outer ear. Fortunately for skin-divers this pressure can be equalised through a flat tube, which connects the ear to the back of the throat, called the Eustachian tube. It can become so

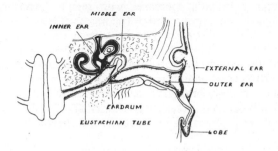

Fig. 1. Diagram of the inner ear showing the eustachian tube which, when opened, equalises pressure between the two sides of the eardrum.

29

clogged up with sticky catarrh mucus that it is effectively sealed. Most people can still manage to "clear" their ears by opening this tube without much trouble, although some divers may find this difficult at first. The technique is to pinch the nose, through the compensator in the diving mask, and then swallow, or blow gently down the nose. After a cold or bad attack of catarrh, ear clearing may present a particular problem but if you have any difficulty diving should be abandoned until the trouble has cleared up. Under no circumstances should a diver try and encourage the tubes to open by blowing with excessive force, as this can do serious damage to the sinuses. Nor must the process of ear clearing be left too late. The open end of the Eustachian canal consists of a shallow trough of stiff cartilage with a soft membrane stretched over it. Under pressure this membrane may be pushed inwards against the cartilage and, if this happens, the only way to clear your ears is to reduce the pressure by finning into shallower water and going through the clearing procedure again. If you just try and force the ears to clear you may perforate your eardrum, allowing water to flood in, or else rupture the lining of the middle ear which will fill with blood and fluid. If the ear drum perforates and water rushes in it will produce sudden giddiness, if the middle ear ruptures you will go temporarily deaf. The latter condition will probably clear up on its own after a few days rest from diving.

All of which is not to strike another alarmist stance but merely to point out the risks and the consequences of not sticking to diving rules, which state simply: Start clearing your ears as soon as you begin the dive, not when they hurt. If you cannot clear easily, especially if this difficulty follows a sinus attack or cold, then return to shallower water and try again. If they still will not clear, abandon the dive.

Cold

This can be an insufficiently appreciated hazard. A wet suit helps to protect the diver by providing insulation, but as I mentioned in the last chapter, during deep dives the insulation value of a neoprene becomes less effective as nitrogen bubbles trapped in the foam are compressed. A diver's tolerance to cold increases with regular exposure to low temperatures and can be improved by training and fitness. However, it is vitally important to realise once you have come to the limits of your own tolerance and end the dive. Early symptoms of the cold are goose pimples, as the body tries to erect hairs to form an insulating barrier, and muscular tremors. If the heat loss persists there will be a blueing of the skin, a slowing down of the breathing and a reduced pulse rate. Hand movements will become increasingly clumsy and the diver will find it more difficult to concentrate and use equipment effectively.

Sight

Because light waves are bent as they pass from water to the air space between your face mask and your eyes, there is a magnifying effect underwater. Everything looks one third bigger or seems to be closer than it really is. At first you may be confused by this phenomena and it can be a problem when taking pictures or shooting cine film underwater as we shall see. However, with a little experience it becomes a simple matter for the diver to make the necessary mental adjustments.

The first sea dive will, quite naturally, lead to anxiety on the part of the newcomer. Even divers with a lot of underwater hours in their log books still feel slightly tense before a dive and this, as I explained, can be beneficial, producing that extra edge of care which reduces the risk of silly mistakes.

There is, however, a fine borderline between a natural anxiety and a state of panic in which the diver behaves in an irrational and often self-destructive way. At first everything is strange. The sounds are strange, the shift in apparent image size, the reduction of contrast, the darkness of northern waters are strange, breathing through the mouth is strange. Add to these unfamiliar sensations unspoken fears such as limb entangling weed and hostile sea creatures, plus the deeper bogies of the subconscious, and you have any number of good reasons for losing self-control.

How enjoyable you find your early dives will depend to a very great extent on the skill and understanding of your instructor. Providing the transition from the familiarity of the baths to open water is made carefully, there is no reason why needless fears should spoil the excitement of that first journey beneath the waves.

It must, however, be said that some divers who are perfectly happy splashing around in pools never really take to open water diving. Perhaps they are slightly claustrophic and fear the shut in feeling of the mask and wet suit, maybe they are just temperamentally unsuited to the sport. Under no circumstances should nervous divers be forced to participate by enthusiastic relatives or friends. If a person is not happy in open water then that fact should be accepted by everybody. There are many enthusiastic club supporters doing invaluable work behind the scenes who have never developed a taste for regular diving. As organisers, equipment officers or lecture room speakers they can still play extremely important roles in diving and in the enjoyment of the sport by their fellow divers.

Even divers who are normally quite happy underwater can get into difficulties through panic. I remember soon after I had started diving, about eight years ago, I was invited on a wreck dive by some friends. When we arrived at the beach the weather was sullen and windy and the bay was extremely choppy. The conditions were not, however, so bad that we considered it necessary to call the dive off. The beach entry was a difficult one over very sharp, shell encrusted rocks. After scrambling down a sheer scarp face into the water, and swimming clear of the breakers which had a nasty habit of flinging one back onto the rocks and then scraping one down them like a piece of cheese on a grating board, I submerged thankfully beside my diving companion. I then discovered that I had a weight problem, I was too negative. This was because my weights were adjusted to compensate for the buoyancy of a full wet suit and, on this dive in tropical waters, I was wearing only a wet suit top. As I then had only a surface life-jacket I was unable to adjust my buoyancy as I might have done with a ABLJ. At that point I should have scrubbed the dive and gone back to the beach to correct the weight belt. Foolishly, I pressed on. The visibility was down to a few feet because the waves, working in shallow water, had churned up the sandy sea bed, and the current was powerful and flowing in the wrong direction. After finning a few hundred yards with negative buoyancy pulling me down, I was getting fairly tired. I should have signalled to my companion and returned, with him, to shore. Once again, although feeling rather worried, I continued. Because of the current and the poor visibility we missed the wreck which lay at 40 feet and went down to 70 feet. At this point my demand valve suddenly ceased to deliver any air.

Even under normal conditions the sudden failure of a demand valve can be a frightening experience. This happened when I was tired, already anxious and in no state to rationalise the situation. I might have taken off for the surface like a missile and possibly have given myself an embolism on the way. Fortunately training, rather than any inbuilt reserves of courage, took over. I attracted the attention of my companion and indicated that I had an air problem and was heading for the surface. He acknowledged and we began to surface. I was now feeling extremely uncomfortable. Realising the seriousness of my position he indicated that we should share air, both taking it in turns to breath from his bottle. However, at thirty feet my own valve began to function sufficiently for me to take a breath. I had, during the ascent, been breathing out steadily to prevent the possibility of an embolism.

On the surface my problems were far from over. The sea was breaking heavily and swamped my snorkel which I was now having to use because the valve had packed up again. My companion had inflated his ABLJ and helped me back to land. I was tired out and my exit was even more of a nightmare than the entry, but I made it back to the beach. After resting for ten minutes, fitting a new valve and correcting my weight problems I returned to complete the dive. It was not an experience I looked forward to, although it turned out a reasonably pleasant dive in the end, but like the pilot who crash lands, and has to fly again right away, I felt that unless I submerged again that day it would be a great deal harder to get back into the water the following day.

The story has a happy ending—we found the wreck—and a number of useful morals.

First, the valve failed because it was a spare which I hadn't bothered to keep regularly serviced. Second, I should have scrubbed the dive at least twice before the valve actually brought things to a dramatic end. Third, having regained the surface feeling extremely winded, I should have

In cold, dark northern waters a diver wearing full protective clothing works on the sea bed. Here a special hydraulic gun is being used to drive steel spikes into the rocks during a survey. (Photo: Cy Conder)

An instructor from Number One Branch of the BSAC demonstrates correct mask fitting procedure. The mask is held in the left hand and all stray hair removed from the forehead. (See chapter four)

The straps are drawn back over the head.

Mask clearing technique being practised in a pool during a BSAC training session. Note the way the mask is held in place while exhaled air blows the water clear. (See chapter four)

dumped at least part of my gear. It was a combination of bad luck and bad judgement—mostly the latter of which I am justifiably ashamed. However, two good things do emerge from the saga. The first is that proper training can help you make the right decisions automatically, and secondly an experienced and calm companion can greatly reduce panic. My diving partner behaved as one would expect a diver of competence to react, decisively and coolly thus reducing my anxieties. When you are diving keep an eye out for your companion and watch for the first signs of panic. Dr Art Bachrac, the Director of Behavioural Sciences of the U.S. Navy Research Centre, has made a close examination of the causes and symptoms of diver panic and suggests the following tell tale danger signs.

Increased breathing, easily detected by the build-up of exhaust bubbles. This can be quite striking. I remember standing on a jetty wall once while some volunteers searched for, and recovered, the body of a seaman who had stumbled drunk into the harbour and drowned. It was easy enough to tell when one of the divers located the body because of the rapid increase in his surface bubbles.

The second give away is when the diver moves from the horizontal swimming position into a more upright posture, clearly preparing to head for the surface. Another posture change may be for the diver to swim with short, jerking leg movements, finning from the knees rather than the thighs. Finally if you see a diver hastily trying to read all his instruments he is probably on the border line of panic. The cure is a calm, assisted return to shallower water, though not necessarily to the surface. It is on the surface that the diver is at his most vulnerable and realising this many have a real fear of the moment of return.

If you feel panic coming on, then try to remember your training, do not rush to the surface. Do not just vanish leaving your companion finning happily and riskily off on his own.

Avoiding panic is easy enough to write about, and easy enough to over-come in the comfort of an armchair. When it strikes one may find it less easy to be objective. The only answer is a self-discipline and confidence which is based on sound training.

There is one final diving hazard which occurs not under the sea but on the surface. Napoleon, who suffered agonies from seasickness, once remarked to a friend: "The British may rule the waves for all I care, but I would to God they could rule them a bit straighter!" Many divers whose day has been ruined by the miseries of sickness would heartily agree. They may take some little comfort from the fact that they are not alone in their suffering. It has been estimated that only about three per cent of people are completely immune to this type of sickness which some doc-tors believe may be caused by the balancing mechanisms being thrown out of gear. The rolling or pitching of a boat produces sickness more regularly than an up and down motion, and a slow rate of pitching tends to be worse than rapid pitching.

It is fashionable to laugh at sea sickness in others, as in the story of a

33

refined woman who asked the captain of her cruise liner what her husband should do in case of sickness. "It's not necessary to tell him Madam," replied the Captain pleasantly. "He'll know!"

There is no need to adopt quite such a negative attitude, as there are ways of reducing sickness. Having hardened my stomach in youth by cross-channel yacht racing and a period spent on an Arctic trawler, I felt fairly immune, until coming back from France last year I suffered the indignity of being violently ill on a cross-channel steamer. In a way I brought this on myself by ignoring the basic rules. I had driven overnight across France and was exhausted. The likelihood of sickness increases with tiredness. I allowed myself to get cold. You should keep warm. I went down to a cabin. You should try and avoid fumes and the shipboard smells associated with confined space. I drank a cup of coffee. Avoid this and beer before going to sea. You should also avoid eating greasy food, a caution which ought not to apply to divers who should never eat a heavy meal of any sort immediately prior to diving.

One tip, if you feel sick on the diving boat, is to ask to take the helm. It sometimes reduces the illness. Also, if possible, kit up as much as possible before you ancor at the diving site. Bending and stooping, concentrating on buckles and fasteners may not be too difficult while the craft is underway, but when anchored it can be extremely sickness provoking. Finally, get into the water as soon as possible as you will feel quite OK once the boat is left behind. On the other hand if you do feel unwell and may vomit then you must call off the dive. Anti-sickness pills can be taken, but their side effects must be carefully considered. Some brands tend to make you sleepy and can cause nitrogen narcosis to affect you at shallower than normal depths. If you have taken a pill then avoid deep dives and be certain to tell your diving companion, and the dive leader that you have done so.

Anti-sickness tablets are either antihistamines or products based on hyoscine. The antihistamines last longest but they also cause drowsiness which varies from person to person. You should test your reaction to this type of tablet while sitting around at home. If one product seems to seriously impair your alertness, try another of the brand names. Antihistamines should be taken a minimum of four hours before the dive.

Antihistamines

Brand Name	Dose	Duration
Marzine, Valoid, Sereen	1	6–8 hours
Dramamine	1	4–6 hours
Avomine	1	4–6 hours
Ancolan	2	12–24 hours
Sealegs	4	
Hyoscine		
Quells, Traveltabs	1–2	$1\frac{1}{2}$–3 hours

Hyoscine is a drug which act on the nerve endings of the stomach and is effective for controlling short term sickness. The tablets should be taken about an hour in advance, although this time can be reduced if necessary. Hyoscine tablets may cause less drowsiness than anti-histamines, but again test the effect they have on you at home and not on a dive.

4

Your Way To The Sea

A properly trained diver should start to enjoy the sport right from his first sea dive. Insufficient training is not merely hazardous but can prevent you from ever getting complete enjoyment from the sport, as a bad fright on an early dive may make you over-anxious and unable to relax underwater.

Training will almost certainly start at the swimming pool, probably with snorkel practice. This is a useful apprenticeship for air-diving, and anybody who feels at home in the water should soon master the art.

Snorkelling—Putting on the Equipment

To fit the face mask, hold it face-plate downwards in your left hand with the strap lying out of the way over the top side of the mask. Push back your hair with the right hand and then press the mask against the face. Now draw the strap over the back of the head. The strap should be long enough for you to slip the snorkel tube under it. In the water the tube should be adjusted so that it is in an upright position when you are looking downwards.

The mask will mist up unless you take the precaution of spitting onto the inside of the glass and then rinsing it out with a little water. If it still has a tendency to mist try wetting the face to cool down the skin.

The flippers will slip on more easily if you rinse them out and wet the feet before fitting.

Snorkelling—Using the Equipment

You are now ready to enter the pool. Walking will be tricky at first, until you get into the habit of waddling slightly to prevent treading on your feet. Gripping the snorkel mouth-piece gently between your teeth, try lying face downwards in the water, gently and smoothly breathing in and out through the tube. Now try swimming the width of the pool. Correct finning technique will produce the maximum amount of propulsion with the minimum effort. Beginners tend to work too hard and splash wildly. Not only is this exhausting bu the disturbance will frighten off marine life for yards around. Keep the legs stretched out, toes pointed and pivot at the hips. Do not worry if you are rather stiff at first, with practice it will be possible to relax the legs, keeping the knees flexed rather than stiff. Be careful that you do not relax so much that you start to "cycle" along as this is a waste of effort.

When you have mastered finning and are happy about moving along the surface, practice a dive. There is no need to be very elegant about this at first but it is worthwhile attempting a smooth duck-dive entry right from the start. This is the best type of entry for divers as it combines maximum depth with the minimum of effort and creates the least disturbance.

To duck-dive, lie flat on the surface of the pool. Bend forward at the waist with your arms pointing straight out in front of you. Now lift both legs together straight up and, at the same moment, sweep the arms sideways in a breast stroke motion. This will take you smoothly and effortlessly to the bottom of the pool. As soon as the open end of the snorkel tube dips beneath the surface it will, of course, fill with water. Some divers close their mouthpiece by simply sticking the tongue against

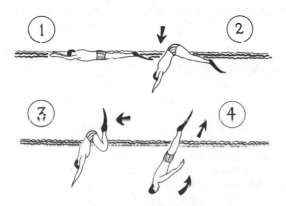

Fig. 2. The correct technique for a duck-dive. (1) Lie flat on the surface. (2) Bend forward at the waist with arms pointing in front of you. (3) Lift both legs together—straight up. (4) You will dive smoothly and effortlessly.

it. A more satisfactory technique, which may take a little practice to master, is to hold the water in the mouth but prevent it getting any further by closing your throat against it. This is a trick, like learning to ride a bicycle, once mastered never forgotten.

After swimming a distance under water, surface with sufficient breath left to expel water from the snorkel by blowing out.

As the routine of diving, finning smoothly and easily along under the surface, and surfacing again, becomes more natural, turn your attention to the ascent. Leaving the depths in a haphazard way can be dangerous. In the pool you may surface under another swimmer, at sea you run the risk of surfacing beneath the diving boat or a fully kitted up diver. Look up and check that the water above you is clear before surfacing.

In early stages of snorkel training you should use the shallow end of the pool. When you dive in deeper water you will feel the pressure against your ear-drums. As I explained, this pain must be relieved at once by clearing the ears. If your ears do not clear and the pain persists then return to the surface.

Before swimming underwater it is perfectly safe to take two deep breaths, but the technique of deep breathing, known as *hyperventilation* should be avoided. The idea behind hyperventilation is to expel as much carbon dioxide from the lungs as possible. There is an organ at the back of the brain which is sensitive to the amount of carbon dioxide in the bloodstream and stimulates the breathing as this level rises. By "scrubbing" carbon dioxide from the system you can temporarily fool the mechanism but this may result in a lack of oxygen which will cause you to black out.

Snorkelling is a necessary diving technique which helps train beginners to relax in shallow water and familiarise themselves the submerging. But it is only a preparation for the equipment dives which are to follow.

Skin Diving (also known as S.C.U.B.A.—self contained underwater breathing apparatus—diving)
If you follow a course of training at a well-organised diving club, preferably a branch of the British Sub Aqua Club or one affiliated to it, then each pool session will include a lecture and demonstration as well as a practical period in the water. By the time you put on diving equipment for the first time you should, therefore, be completely familiar with it and understand the potential dangers. In the pool the only real risk, if the deep end is ten feet or more, is of an air embolism, and as I explained in the previous chapter, this hazard is easily avoided.

The first difficulty you encounter may simply be one of staying on the bottom, or coming up at will. This is a question of correctly adjusting your buoyancy by wearing the right number of weights. If you find yourself crawling around the bottom of the pool then you are negatively buoyant. If you find it hard to submerge at all then you are positively buoyant. The correct state of neutral buoyancy is one in which you can control your rise and fall by merely breathing in or out. To achieve this, adjust the weights until you can lie on the bottom of the pool, take a breath and rise gently, then fall again as you exhale.

How comfortable and easy you feel underwater will depend on your getting the equipment correctly adjusted and making sure all the straps are tight. To test the adjustment of the cylinder back-pack try one or two forward and backward somersaults to see if it stays put.

Whilst diving it is quite possible to knock your face mask out of place and flood it with water. Even if this accident never happens to you, worn seals or poorly tightened straps may cause a slow seepage of sea into the bottom of the mask. Either way do not panic as this water is very easily removed. Simply hold the mask firmly against the face by pressing on the top edge, with the head and body in a vertical position. Lift the lower edge of the mask just clear of the face, and breath out sharply. The water will immediately be blown clear.

Open Water Diving
With pool training completed, you are ready for the first open water dive, either in the sea or in some fresh water training area such as a lake, or flooded quarry.

Some divers find the transition from the clear familiar and safe waters of the swimming pool to these darker regions difficult. If your instructor knows his job, he should be able to instil that much needed little bit of extra confidence. With some divers over confidence may be the problem. Because they found swimming pool training so easy they tend to be unprepared mentally for the very different conditions.

Never, under any circumstances, make the first open water dive alone or with an inexperienced diver. If you feel very unhappy about the prospect then don't dive. Nobody should ever force themselves to dive, it is suppossed to be an enjoyable sport not a form of torture, nor should they press somebody who is reluctant to dive against their will. Before any dive you should feel perfectly fit and rested. It is a bad idea to drive through the night then take to the water still exhausted from the journey. Do not dive if you have a cold or a hangover!

Check your equipment carefully. The dive leader should do this for you as well, but it is never a good idea to rely entirely on anybody else, not even your instructor. Make sure the harness on the back-pack is correctly adjusted and fits comfortably. Make sure that all the quick release catches move freely and easily, remember you may be trying to free the equipment with numbed fingers.

Check the amount of air in the bottle. At first you will waste air by over-breathing, so even at the shallow depths reached during early dives you may use air very fast. If you have a life-jacket with adjustable buoyancy then make sure the compressed air bottle is fully charged. Be very cautious about using this equipment to alter buoyancy under the surface during early dives.

The life-jacket goes on first then the back-pack, bottle and the weight belt. This order is dictated by a possible emergency on the surface in which it might be necessary to jettison some or all of the equipment. The first thing you will want to lose is the weight belt followed by the bottle and demand valve. On no account fasten the weight belt in such a way that it prevents the life-jacket from being inflated.

At the diving site the non-diver in charge of the boat will anchor and raise the diving flat. On a properly organised first sea dive some of the party will provide snorkel cover, checking on the divers progress by following the bubbles of expelled air, and helping them back to the diving boat in case of trouble. The spot chosen for the dive will probably be one familiar to the more experienced divers, who will know about problems of currents and the best time to dive. If it takes place over rocks so much the better, there is nothing more boring than to dive on featureless sand or mud, and the visibility over rocks is going to be better.

Now comes the moment which the weeks of training and lectures have been leading up to. Make sure that you are happy with the adjustment of your equipment. Rinse out your mask with some saliva and sea water and place it in position. Some divers go over the side with the snorkel tube in place and fit their mouth piece in the water. For the first few dives I advise you to go in with the mouth-piece in place and delivering air. It is less alarming, means you have nothing more to do once you are in the water and ensures that the cylinder is turned on before you go over the side. I know of several divers who have pushed their mouthpieces into place once in the sea only to discover that the bottle was firmly in the off position!

From a small boat the safest method of entering the water is backwards. Hold onto your mask, to prevent it being displaced, and roll gently into the sea. For a few seconds the world will become a confusion of sensations, cold as the sea seeps into your wet suit, a mixture of strange, distorted sounds, your own breathing, the slap of water against the side of the diving boat, the movement of other divers close by. Light and dark, emerald green and deeper, bottle green shading off into the darkness below, alternate as you turn over in the water. A trail of gleaming saucer shaped bubbles stream to the surface and you follow them, breaking back into the world of air and sky a few yards from the diving boat.

Your diving companion will fin over and check that everything is OK. Now you are ready to explore the mystery of a world about which man knows less than the surface of the moon. A duck-dive takes you back beneath the surface, following the darkening shape of your partner and his trail of phosphorescent bubbles into the gloom. Do not swim too close or his fins may dislodge your mask, nor so far away that you lose him. If either of these problems happen there is no need for panic. In the pool you will have been trained to take off you mask, replace it and clear out the water. If you lose your diving partner then surface calmly, remembering to breath correctly. On the surface remain cool, orientate yourself with the shoreline or the diving boat. If you feel out of breath or tired then inflate the life-jacket. In a few moments your diving companion should have surfaced to find you.

Because it is easy to lose one's bearings when diving in the poor visibility often found around European coasts, it is useful to follow a line, perhaps the anchor rope, or a buoy line, down to the sea bed. Arrival at the bottom may well take you by surprise. One moment you will be finning through shifting layers of green-greyness, in which plankton and free floating weeds drift lazily with the current, then the uneven floor of the sea will be upon you. Freed from gravity you can drift eagle-like above the ocean floor. An underwater cliff appears and you glide down it after your diving companion, following the tumbled scree of rocks and boulders, then turning to retrace your path over the rocky outcrop, and rising back to the surface world. With luck and good navigation the diving boat will be only a short swim away.

Navigation

As you grow more experienced you will want to explore further afield and dive deeper. Now it will be necessary to acquire some skill in underwater navigation and learn how to use a compass.

Disorientation is frequent, even for experienced divers, in poor visibility. On land we have a number of clues which help us to locate our position in relation to other objects. Our sense of balance tells us our position in relation to the earth, sight and hearing provide other important clues. Underwater none of these will be of much help. In water sound travels at more than twice its speed in air (4,700 feet per second in water, 1,090 feet per second in air) which makes it almost impossible to tell from which direction a sound is coming. The body mechanisms responsible for balance and posture have no part to play underwater. The eyes are confused by the lack of colours and the change in contrast. It is possible to get so confused that you can't tell whether you are diving up or down, swimming towards the shore or away from it, or simply finning around in circles. Sometimes not even the upward flight of your bubbles can provide the clue because the murky water makes it impossible to see them.

The sea itself provides one source of navigation aids, technology has given us others, ranging from a reliable compass which costs a few pounds to the extremely complex and sophisticated electronic aids which I shall discuss in Chapter Twelve. The first rule in poor visibility is never to dive without some static point of reference to the sea bed. This may be the anchor line, a buoy rope or a sinker especially laid down to act as a reference mark.

On the bottom use this reference point as a base marker and then guide yourself across the sea floor by noting landmarks, boulders with distinctive shapes or, in an isolated position, unusually shaped outcrops of rock. When navigating across sand note the direction of the wave ripples, when navigating across vegetation—a very difficult seascape—you may be able to note the direction in which the current moves the weed fronds. But this is at best an uncertain guide and you are much safer using a good compass.

If you want to make out a route along the sea floor, perhaps to guide other divers to a wreck site, then this is easily done by taking down empty bottles and anchoring them on a length of line with suitable weights or pieces of rock. A quick squirt of air into the neck of each, to force out the water, and you have a marker which will last for some considerable time. In poor visibility these can be made even more noticeable by covering in a day-glo plastic material.

A compass should be chosen with an eye to reliability rather than cheapness. Buy one which has a liquid damped needle for accuracy. When using the compass don't forget that ferrous metal will affect the needle and give an incorrect reading, so watch out for the steel cylinders of your companion or metal on a wreck. When taking the reading hold the compass at eye level in the centre of your line of travel and make certain that your whole body is lined up in this direction. If your body is at an angle and you correct for this merely by turning your head then you will be well of course at the end of the swim.

Surface navigation is clearly of equal importance and any divers who intend to go more than a few hundred yards from shore should have an experienced boat handler with them and a craft capable of carrying all the equipment and members of the team without any risk of overloading. Safety equipment should include a secondary mean of propulsion, oars or sail, signal flares in good working order, and a first aid kit. Flasks of hot coffee will be extremely welcome after a dive and can be useful in combating the cold, but alcohol should never be offered to anybody who has got really cold.

Before setting off check the weather forecast and the tides. If the area is unfamiliar to you then ask local fishermen or the coastguard about any problems with currents.

Deep Dives

For a diver who normally explores around the forty feet depth, a dive to eighty feet should be considered as carefully as a dive to over a hundred feet by a diver whose experience is confined to the eighty foot mark. Deep dives must only be undertaken after careful planning and a consideration of the psychological and physiological problems.

As we saw in the previous chapter, physiological hazards of breathing air under pressure increase the deeper we dive. At depths below eighty feet there is a risk of nitrogen narcosis "rapture of the deep", which will make a diver act in an unpredictable and quite probably self-destructive manner. During an ascent there is the risk of the "bends" (nitrogen forming bubbles in the bloodstream) unless decompression procedures are observed. This means spending a certain amount of time at different depths to allow the nitrogen to pass out of the tissues. What decompression stops you must make, and for what period, are to be found in published Decompression Tables. These have been worked out by the Royal Navy and by the Navies of other countries, and vary in the stops they demand and the amount of time which they say can be spent at depths without any decompression stages becoming necessary. Some divers feel that the R.N. tables are on the conservative side. You still do well to follow them at first rather than select another set of figures which appear to allow you longer at the depths. Such dives should only be made in the company of experienced divers who are able to recognise the symptoms of both nitrogen narcosis and decompression sickness, and know what steps to take if these occur. A minor bend can be treated by immediate resubmersion to a suitable depth, a major bend which, I must emphasise again, should only occur as the result of a major piece of bad luck or stupidity, will need immediate treatment in a recompression chamber.

When deep diving you should keep an even more watchful eye on your companion than usual. It will be helpful if you know him well, both above and below the surface, so that you immediately become aware of any personality changes. Narcosis tends to make divers behave in an exuberant manner, but somebody who is naturally exuberant may just be himself rather than the victim of the narcs. A rather retiring personality who suddenly becomes erratic in his manner is easier to detect.

Deep diving is more anxiety provoking than dives in shallower, clearer water and the threshold of diver panic is probably lower. It has also been shown that there is a connection between diver anxiety and the onset of nitrogen narcosis.

I have already mentioned that during deep dives compression of the trapped bubbles causes neoprene wet suit material to become a less effective insulator. Equally important it also becomes less buoyant. A diver who is correctly weighted in shallow water may find himself as much as 15 lbs overweight at 100 feet. The only way to correct this negative buoyancy is by means of an adjustable life-jacket.

From this brief outline of the hazards in deep diving you will see that it is a challenge which should only be considered by experienced divers who have a clear idea of the problems and dangers involved. Nobody should ever dive deep out of a false sense of bravado. As Reg Vallintine, the Director General of the British Sub Aqua Club said in *Diver* magazine: "There are still parts of the world where misguided individuals still believe that the deepest aqualung diver is the best. The sad record of their deaths bears witness to the futility of this form of underwater Russian roulette."

What does make a good diver? In the same article Reg admirably summed up the attributes which every diver should aim for if he is to get the maximum enjoyment from his sport, and become a valued and trusted member of a diving club. "You will start to recognise the good diver as soon as he arrives" says Reg, "because he will have the right equipment for the particular dive he is going to do. He'll always have reliable safety aids too—ABLJ, pressure gauge, depth gauge, knife, snorkel tube and enough spare "O" rings to supply his own needs and those of others if necessary.

"A good diver keeps his equipment in good order too and will be the first to wash it off in fresh water after the dive.

"In the boat or on the shore before diving, he is cheerful and confident without feeling the need to tell everyone of the 'hairy' happenings during his last immersion.

"His preparation for diving will be fast but methodical and he will be very aware of the state of other divers, patiently offering advice and help and checking his companion's equipment and quick releases.

"He will also be the one who keeps a careful eye on the weather, the sea conditions and the way the cox or skipper is handling the boat.

"He will not be afraid to cancel a dive if conditions are not right or cheerfully to abide by the decision of a dive leader who has done so.

"Once in the water he is the diver who seldom if ever gets separated from his companion, although he doesn't do this by roping up to him or constantly interrupting him with signals.

"His sense of underwater orientation will tell him the way back to the boat if it is anchored, and the position of the other divers in his group.

"He will not merely 'hare off' and stuff his sack with underwater goodies, but will point out to you those things of interest he sees.

"If the dive is deep, he will be checking your signals for evidence of narcosis. Underwater, he will move slowly and easily with a minimum of effort, but will be fit enough to fin strongly against a current if necessary. His weights will have been carefully prepared to keep him as near neutrally buoyant as possible.

"The good diver looks ahead and you will find him automatically checking your pressure gauge towards the end and asking if you are suffering from cold.

"When you leave the bottom, he will close up and watch you like a hawk because he knows that the ascent and swim back is the most dangerous part of the dive.

"Good 'water sense' evolves from environmental awareness, thinking ahead, and prior diving experience with a seasoned veteran.

"Back on board or ashore he will check that all divers have returned and will discuss the dive with you in a knowledgeable but unboring way before entering up his log.

"To sum up, I think you could say that the good diver is the safe diver, the careful diver, and the diver who you feel instinctively is ready and able to help you when you really need it.

"Above all, let's remember one thing about them—all good divers arrive alive!"

Section Two

5

Underwater Photography—Problems and equipment

A camera underwater is not a cumbersome luxury; for the scientific diver, archaeologist, biologist or wreck hunter it is an essential tool for recording important evidence *in situ,* and for enabling a far more detailed and careful surface examination to be made of artifacts, sites and specimens. For the sports diver too the camera is a valuable aid to enjoyment, preserving the highlights of memorable dives for the winter evenings. It is hardly surprising, therefore, that in a recent survey, carried out by the British Sub Aqua Club, into activities which divers wanted to take up once they had gained underwater experience, photography was listed as the number one interest.

There are two main types of underwater photography. The average camera user, who wants to get the best results possible with easily used and relatively inexpensive equipment. Then there is the more professional user, who may be after accurate scientific recordings, publication of his work in magazines or simply the highest possible quality underwater. Such divers must be prepared to outlay considerable time and a fair amount of money to achieve their ambitions.

Because the aims of these groups are rather different, and to avoid confusing readers of limited photographic experience with a mass of technical information, which is quite unnecessary if you are only interested in producing reasonable pictures under fair to good conditions, I have divided this subject into two sections. Here I shall outline the basic problems confronting the underwater photographer and examine the ways in which cameras can be taken beneath the surface. In the following chapter I shall look at more sophisticated techniques and discuss the latest housings and accessories.

THE PROBLEMS

Effects of water on light
We have already noted that light is selectively absorbed when it passes through water. The longer wavelengths, red and orange are absorbed first, which is why the sea looks blue. In clear water conditions, such as you get in the Pacific all red is absorbed at a depth of 20 feet [7 m] while orange disappears at 35 feet [12 m] and yellow is filtered out at 65 feet [21 m]. By the time you reach 100 feet [33 m] the whole scene takes on a blue-grey appearance. This presents the photographer with two

problems. Firstly the brilliant colours of much marine life can only be revealed if some form of artificial light is used. Secondly the light lost through this absorption cuts down the amount available to make exposures.

Light is not only lost through absorption. A fair amount is reflected back from the surface of the sea, especially under choppy conditions, and by the scattering effect of suspended material, plankton, weed, animal life, etc. This scattering not only reduces the amount of available light, it also lowers the subject contrast and makes it more difficult to get pictures with high definition.

In British waters visibility ranges from around 60 feet [20 m] to zero, whilst in the Mediterranean it is possible to get 100 feet [33 m] or more. Conditions are naturally best when the sea is calm and the sun directly overhead, because the least amount of light is being lost through surface reflection. But even so the underwater photographer spends his life taking pictures under conditions which the surface cameraman would regard as working in fog.

Apart from these absorption and scattering effects, the difference in the refractive indices between air and water presents yet another difficulty. I have already mentioned that objects seen through the diving mask appear to be a third larger, and therefore closer, than they are. The same effect can be observed when a straight rod is placed in a glass sided fish tank, it appears to bend because the submerged image looks larger than the in-air image.

A camera in a housing, its lens viewing the underwater scene through an airspace and a transparent window, sees objects in exactly the same way as the masked eyes of the diver. This means that surface calibrated focusing scales are no longer accurate and new ones have to be worked out. However, this problem will be overcome if you are using a reflex camera, either single-lens or twin-lens, as the light reaching the divers eyes as he focuses is refracted to exactly the same extent as the light which reaches the film when the photograph is taken.

Refraction also affects the angle of coverage of the lens, increasing its apparent focal length. (Those unfamiliar with these and other technical terms used in the next two chapters will find a full explanation in Appendix Three.) If you have a lens of 50 mm focal length, i.e. a standard lens on a 35 mm camera, it will apparently increase its focal length by one third underwater turning it into a slightly long focus (73 mm lens). In the same way a lens which is wide angle on the surface, for example a 35 mm focal length lens used on 35 mm film, becomes almost a standard lens underwater. There are ways of overcoming this problem which I shall discuss in the next chapter.

We can summarise the problems so far discussed as follows.
1) Underwater, light is reduced by absorption and surface reflection. This makes longer exposures, necessary, and also changes the colour of objects underwater, red being the worst affected.

48

A girl student learns mask clearing under the watchful eye of an expert BSAC instructor from Number One Branch.

A girl student practises sharing air in the pool during a training session. (See chapter four)

An underwater training session in progress during a BSAC bath night. The instructor is showing trainee divers how to remove their equipment underwater. (See chapter four)

A diver heads for the surface after a dive to more than 160 feet in the Mediterranean. (See chapter four)

2) Suspended matter between the camera and subject reduces contrast and image definition.

3) Lenses lose some of the covering power [i.e.: how wide a view they can cover] when being used in underwater cases which have flat points.

4) The object appears to be larger and closer because of underwater magnification. This means that surface distance markings engraved on the lens are inaccurate.

The solution is to use a camera with as wide an angle lens as possible. Most cheap cameras, for instance, the Instamatics, have a non-interchangeable standard lens. This means they are unsuitable for serious underwater photography and will only give reasonable results down to depths of ten or fifteen feet in clear water for general picture taking. If, however, you are using one of these cameras with flash and a close-up lens to make studies of marine life, preferably static marine life, where your subject/lens working distance is no more than a couple of feet, they will produce reasonable results at much greater depths.

Even when using wide-angle lens it is essential to work in as close to the subject as possible because of the loss of sharpness caused by suspended material and light scattering. As a general rule you will get good results up to a quarter of the distance you can easily see. In other words, if you are working in the Mediterranean with 60 foot [20 m] visibility then you will be able to get good pictures of objects 15 feet [5 m] away and excellent ones of anything closer. If on the other hand, you are working in English waters with four feet of visibility then anything you try to shoot beyond a foot distance is going to produce disappointing results.

Exposure

The easiest way of getting exposures right is to use a meter. These can be bought, starting at a modest sum, complete in underwater cases. Alternatively a cheap selenium cell meter which takes a direct reading (the needle moving against an f-stop scale) can be completely encapsulated in a block of perspex. This means that once the meter has been set at a selected ASA speed and moulded into the block it is there for ever. You cannot make any changes in the speed setting and if the meter goes wrong you have to throw it away. I used one of these meters designed by scientist/diver Brian Ray in the Mediterranean and found it completely accurate and easy to manipulate. If you shoot a great deal of colour then a meter is really essential and will soon pay for its outlay in saved exposures.

However, using any type of meter requires care because of the light scattering effects of water. The same applies to automatic cameras which have built-in meters working directly on shutter or f-stop settings. Always take readings from as close to the subject as possible even if this means finning in to make a reading and the finning back to the camera taking position. There are a number of situations where meters can be fooled into suggesting, or automatically setting, too small an f-stop on too high a shutter speed. In both cases the film will be under exposed. Black and white prints will be thin and lacking in detail, colour transparencies too dark. One such situation arises when you are taking a picture of divers on their way to the surface. Here so much light will be coming from around the subjects that meters will be inaccurate. So fin in and then back again. But note that fully automatic cameras cannot be used in this way as they will merely readjust their settings when you return to the taking position. One solution is to set the film speed scale on your automatic camera at a lower rating than you would normally use.

For example, if you put in a roll of TRI-X rated at 400 ASA you should set the meter to 160 ASA. This means it would over-expose every frame by one stop. Where under-exposure due to confusing light was a problem this would help balance things out. Frames which were over-exposed could be corrected at the printing stage. Where colour is concerned this system might well fall down, and experiments with different angles, subjects and speed settings will be needed to discover the right combinations.

Lacking a meter you may find the following table a helpful guide to the exposures needed when using 400 ASA film (i.e. Kodak Tri-X) in the camera. These figures are for British waters with a calm sea and the sun high in the sky. Shutter speed 1/125th sec.

DEPTH		CONDITIONS	
	Sand	Open Water	Rocks/Weeds
6 ft.	f16	f11	f8
10 ft.	f11	f8	f5.6
30 ft.	f5.6	f4	f2

Regard these settings only as a guide and ring important exposures by shooting at one f-stop above and one f-stop below.

When light levels are low you must either use a slow shutter speed or a wide f-stop, often a combination of both, to obtain a correctly exposed picture. As you open up the f-stop you reduce your depth of field. On land, where depth of field is essential and the light levels are low, you can sometimes use a tripod and give a long exposure. Underwater this is usually impossible. I *have* seen photographers using tripods on the sea bed and giving lengthy exposures on completely static subjects, but normally subject movement precludes such a course.

When using speeds of 1/30th or 1/60th be very careful how you take the pictures, because lack of sharpness due to camera movement is very real danger. Squeeze the shutter rather than derk it and be sure to hold the camera steady. When taking pictures it is important to get your buoyancy example right, if you are unable to maintain a required position without a lot of finning the picture is far more likely to be unsharp. Avoid vigorous movement near sandy or muddy sea beds as sediment once disturbed takes a considerable time to settle and may make photography impossible.

Film

In British waters use as fast a film as possible, such as Tri-X which also tends to be a slightly contrasty film and helps when working in low contrast underwater conditions. It can be given extra development to increase the manufacturers normal speed rating of 400 ASA. As you increase speed you also push up contrast, which may not be a bad thing, and increase the grain size which can be a disadvantage because it causes loss of image definition. You should, however, be able to at least double the speed (800 ASA) without noticeable grain problems providing that you process the film carefully. This means doing it yourself as most laboratories will tend to treat the film in rather too cavalier a manner. Keep every solution—developer, stop bath, fix and wash water within plus or minus 1°F of each other. This is especially important with the final wash. Plunging a film from developer or fix at around 68°F into cold wash water causes the silver halide grains, which compose the image, to clump and so increases grain size.

Overseas, where conditions are better, you can use a slower film, Plus-X or Ilford FP4, for example, and still get useable exposure levels.

When shooting colour come in as close to the subject as possible in order to reduce to a minimum the amount of light absorbing water through which the picture has to be taken. I shall discuss flash techniques a little later. It is also possible to use colour correcting filters underwater and these will be considered in the next chapter.

From a point of view of exposure alone a fast colour film is best in British waters. Kodak High Speed Ektachrome is normally rated at 160 ASA, but it can be uprated to 400 ASA without any problems provided it is processed by a laboratory prepared to undertake this work. If necessary High Speed Ektachrome can be pushed to 800 ASA or even 1000 ASA. Although the manufacturers will not take any responsibility for the way their emulsion behaves when treated in this manner, I have seen excellent slides taken underwater with the film rated at 1000 ASA. The only drawback was a slight increase in grain size.

Composition

If you are using a non-reflex camera with a frame-finder mounted at some distance above the lens, then you may suffer from some parallax problems. This is the incorrect framing of subjects due to the different angles of coverage by the lens and finder. Some correction can be achieved by angling the finder slightly downwards, but you may still find early shots are lost when working in close. A subject which appears to have been perfectly central in the finder will vanish out of the top of the print. Experience is the best guide and parallax can be quickly mastered. When using a single lens reflex, of course, there are no parallax problems as the diver/photographer is composing his shot through the lens which takes the picture.

When taking pictures of other divers it is important to include air bubbles, in order to give an impression of the sea around them. Also try to avoid very black (due to light absorption) or bright silver (due to reflection) mask-face plates. It is easier to get details of the diver's features when using flash.

Framing pictures is just as effective beneath the surface as it is on land. When viewing photographs our eyes pass from dark areas to light areas, and so an arch of rocks, for example, with divers swimming between them is especially effective as it leads the eye into the main part of the picture.

Flash Photography

Because of light level and absorption problems, flash is frequently used underwater. Bulb guns provide a relatively cheap and easily transported source of light. A flash bulb will fire underwater because it contains its own air supply, and only the battery and capacitator need to be protected from the sea. Electronic flash housings are available and the advantage of this form of lighting is that it provides a high speed source which freezes movement. It requires a greater initial outlay, although each shot works our far cheaper.

Calculating flash exposures underwater can be something of a problem and, because of light scatter from suspended matter, large areas cannot be illuminated. Some photographers dislike flash pictures because they produce unnatural looking results with subjects starting up against very black backgrounds. Ways of overcoming this problem outlined in the next chapter, involve extra cost and more complex techniques.

You can calculate flash exposures, as on land (by using the flash factor and dividing it by the distance from light source to subject) but reducing the flash factor by one third to take into account loss by absorption.

For example, suppose you are shooting with a bulb which has a factor of 160, at ten feet from the subject. On land this would give an f-stop of f-16. Underwater, reducing the factor by one third, we get approximately 90. The calculated underwater f-stop is, therefore f-9. As this setting doesn't appear on the aperture scales of most cameras we would use the nearest one, i.e. f-8.

The best teacher is again experience and you should keep records of the subject-camera distance and f-stops used so that you can see which exposures worked and which led to over or under exposed results.

When using colour underwater shoot with clear bulbs rather than the blue bulbs which you would use on the surface as the sea will act as a filter for the red part of the bulbs light output.

Cameras and Housings

There is one camera, the Japanese Nikonos which can be taken underwater with no protective case. This ingenious camera is popular with many photographers, especially divers who want a light, easily used and transported camera for record photography. The Nikonos costs about £140 new, but you can frequently find secondhand models in good order

SUMMARY OF PROBLEMS AND SOLUTIONS

Problem	Solution
Colours selectively absorbed by sea.	Use flash or tungsten lamps to show marine life in full colours.
Light lost by absorption scattering and suspended material.	Use fast film to achieve satisfactory exposure level. Use flash or tungsten lights to boost levels. Take light readings in close to subject.
Contrast and definition reduced by suspended material.	Work in as close as possible. Use wide angle lens to include as much of subject as possible at close range.
Refraction upsets focus scale.	Make a new scale with suitable corrections. Use single lens reflex camera.
Refraction reduces covering power of lens.	Use wide angle lens if possible. With standard lens work in close. (See also dome ports in next chapter).
Low shutter speeds may cause camera shake.	Use no speed lower than 1/30th. Squeeze the shutter release, do not jab it. Have buoyancy correctly adjusted.
Parallax problems caused by finder and lens seeing different parts of subject.	Gain experience with frame finder. Have it slightly angled. Use a single lens reflex camera.

for about £80. You can also pick up a much earlier version of this camera, the Calypsophot, for about half the cost of a secondhand Nikonos. However, spares for this model can be a problem. Before buying, check the inside carefully to make sure it has never been flooded. Operate the shutter/wind-on mechanism a number of times to see that they are smooth and free from corrosion. Examine the lens by removing it from the camera and opening up the f-stop fully. Check the f-stop and focus controls, although these are much less likely to show any signs of corrosion or wear. Finally look at the state of the two "O" rings seals which make the camera watertight. It is also a good idea to check out the general external appearance of the camera, as this gives an indication of the way in which it has been treated. The Nikonos can be fitted with a number of accessories for close-up or very wide angle photography.

A Nikonos aside the only answer is to buy or construct a housing for your land camera. Bearing in mind the limitations mentioned earlier, any camera, from the cheapest Instamatic upwards can be used to take underwater pictures. Before considering what type of camera to take underwater it is important to think about the sort of results which you need. There is always a risk of cases leaking and cameras being flooded. Although it is possible to salvage them, a technique which I will discuss in the next chapter, a flooded camera is at best a nuisance and at worst a costly write-off. You should therefore think hard before popping an expensive camera into a perspex box and going over the side with it.

Underwater you just do not need many of the sophistication which an expensive camera provides for the landbased photographer. Because of light levels, for example, there is little point in having a high top shutter speed. You will probably get all the shots you need at between 1/60 and 1/250th second, and the 1/500 and 1/1000 settings on an expensive camera will remain unused as will the speeds below 1/30th second.

A second feature of expensive cameras is the high optical quality. This *can* be extremely important underwater as well, but if you never intend to enlarge your shots more than enprint or half-plate (4.75 × 6.5) size, then there is no point in taking them with a very costly lens. In other words balance the risk to the camera, or the cost of buying such a camera for underwater photography, with your requirements. It may be that a secondhand 35 mm camera or one of the cheaper models, will serve your purpose just as well.

However, a word of warning is necessary here. Not every camera is capable of being used in an underwater housing. The problem is one of linking the camera controls, focus, f-stop setting, shutter release and film transport, with external controls protruding through the case via watertight seals. All such linkages must be straightforward, to prevent anything going wrong at the crucial moment, just when you have lined up a prize winning picture in the viewfinder fifty feet under, for example! External controls must be large and easy to operate even with fingers that may be cold and numb or covered in rubber diving gloves.

If you are a reasonably competent do-it-yourselfer there is no reason why you should not design and build your own underwater housing thus making a considerable saving. There are firms which will supply you with all the necessary materials, professionally designed assemblies, linkages and controls as well as providing advice about the correct ways of putting the case together. Before discussing these construction techniques, we should look at two reasonably priced, commercially available cases to see the type of housings available, which, including the camera, are not too expensive. In Chapter Seven I will discuss more sophisticated housings which, on their own, cost several hundreds of pounds.

The Konica Marine C35

This outfit consists of a camera with 38 mm lens and a plastic housing with carrying strap. The camera uses standard 35 mm film casettes and is completely automatic. A cadium sulphide light meter controls the shutter speeds varying them from between 1/30th and 1/650th second depending on the light levels. This is satisfactory for simple snapshooting at shallow depths. It removes the need for a separate meter and limits the number of external controls.

The housing is constructed from two sections of moulded perspex held together by four captive bolts. The material is ribbed for extra strength and said to be safe down to 120 feet [40 m]. The camera lens looks out through a glass port which can be unscrewed from the perspex mount. Glass has the advantage of being easier to clean and scratching less easily than perspex, which is useful as a scratched viewing port causes loss of definition. However, perspex does not shatter while glass does, which means this case must be treated carefully when near rocks or when exploring wrecks as it would be all too easy to flood the case. Two controls are mounted at the front of the housing and one, the film transport lever, on the top. All the controls are large and easily operated under diving conditions. However, the focusing design is less satisfactory. On land the Konica is focused by means of a range-finder, but this cannot be used underwater because one of the viewing windows of the finder is obscured by the case. Manual setting against the focus scale is necessary and the figures are a little hard to see in poor visibility. There is a frame finder for composition and special synchronisation contacts inside the case allow flash to be used.

The Canon M70
The camera takes 126 cartridge packs which slot into place. The case is entirely made out of perspex. As with the Konica, exposure is automatic and works by varying shutter speeds. The actual speed selected can be seen in the view finder. Film transport is automatic, by means of an electric motor, which cuts down the number of controls needed on the outside of the case. There is, in fact, only a shutter release, a large, ribbed lever mounted on the front of the case. Focus has to be set before sealing the camera into its case. However, this is no real disadvantage, given the simplicity of the equipment and the range of subjects which can be covered using it. With the lens set at about 6 feet [2 m] a wide range of general snapshooting is possible. Both these cameras are best suited to clear waters and provide for example an easy to use means of recording Mediterranean dives and taking land snapshots as well.

Constructing Your Own Case
There are two approaches. You can build a suitably designed box housing out of sheets of perspex, the $\frac{1}{2}''$ thickness being most popular, or you can base your design on a perspex cylinder. Both systems require careful planning and construction to prevent them shattering or leaking under pressure. Whichever system you use it will be useful to practice by constructing small boxes using off-cuts of perspex to gain experience in the techniques of cutting and glueing.

Box Designs

Drawings are first made so that the exact measurements of the case can be accurately worked out and the best position for the external controls must be ease and convenience of operation. The sheets of perspex are best cut to size by the firm from which you buy them. Before glueing ensure that the surfaces are clean and grease free by wiping with some cotton wool soaked in methylated spirits. Strips of Selotape may be used to mask the perspex and prevent the glue from spreading. Surplus glue should be wiped off with a clean cloth. Some constructors prefer to clamp joints after glueing, others claim that the perspex will settle into a perfectly sound joint under its own weight. After practicing making joints using perspex off-cuts you can make up your own mind about the best method for you.

Cements

Perspex Cements

There are many cements suitable for bonding Perspex to itself, but the strength, weathering properties, resistance to attack by moisture, gap filling properties, and resultant appearance of the joint vary considerably with the type of cement used. Obviously for underwater housing construction, the joints must be capable of withstanding considerable loads and must not deteriorate in contact with sea water. Solvents such as chloroform, ethylene dichloride, etc. should not be used for outside or load bearing joints. These compounds are merely solvents of Perspex and have no gap filling properties. Surfaces joined by this means must be machined to an accuracy of 0.001″. The resultant joint can be very clear and attractive, but outdoor exposure may cause the joint to whiten and eventually fail.

Tensol cements have been specially developed to meet particular requirements.

Tensol No. 6 This is a single component liquid, with limited gap filling properties. Its use should be limited to the inside of enclosures (not in contact with sea water). The joint produced is attractive and has moderate bond strength.

Tensol No. 7 This is a two component cement:

Compound A Syrup

Compound B Liquid

The components are mixed in the proportion A:B = 25:1 immediately prior to cementing. It has good gap filling properties and produces a joint of high bond strength. The joint is unaffected by sea water, does not deteriorate with time, and should be used for all external and load bearing joints.

IMPORTANT NOTE: Tensol Cements are highly inflammable and have a low Flash Point. Always keep away from naked flames and store in a well stoppered bottle in a cool place. The shelf life of Tensol No. 6 and No. 7

(Component A) is about 9 months. Tensol No. 7 (Component B) lasts indefinitely. Tensol which has become thick and viscous through are or excessive evaporation (by leaving the bottle unstopped) should be discarded.

Construction Techniques

One of the most experienced designers of perspex housings in Britain is Peter Salmon, who runs a company called Aquamatic at Hitchin in Hertfordshire. As well as supplying custom built housings for cameras and flash units, he sells all the materials and other components needed by the do-it-yourself enthusiast. His full address is listed at the end of this section. I am indebted to Peter for the following hints on home construction. They are best on his systems, which involve perspex cylinders. However, the tips on working perspex apply to whatever type of housing you wish to construct.

Having chosen your camera, the first step is to determine the diameter and length of tubing required. It is essential to take some care before ordering this, the most expensive and most important item of your housing.

The following rules should be conformed to:

1. The greatest diagonal dimension of the camera while looking at the lens must be less that the internal diameter of the tubing. With lever wind cameras you must allow for the arc described by this part while operating.

2. Use the smallest diameter tubing which will clear all operative parts (However, if you intend to fit exposure meter, electronic flash etc. at a later date take this into consideration). *Note*: Obviously the larger the diameter, the more ballast will be required to obtain neutral buoyancy, and the constructor who is considering regular air trips abroad should take this into account. For a really compact housing one of the small $\frac{1}{2}$ frame 35 mm cameras such as Yashica 72E is ideal.

3. Measure for length of tubing with the lens fully extended and lever wind control at its maximum backwards position. Add an extra $\frac{1}{4}$—$\frac{1}{2}$" for clearance. Do NOT allow the lens to touch the front plate as the slight dishing effect under pressure could damage the camera and throw controls out of alignment. The next step is to rigidly mount the camera in position inside the tubing. Three methods are now suggested (mounting camera on rear plate is not recommended due to slight movements by compression of 'O' ring under pressure).

Method 1. This method is suitable for most 35 mm cameras. A piece of flat perspex ($\frac{3}{8}$" thick) is bevelled along the edges (easily done by filing) and cemented in position across the tubing, using Tensol 7. Before cementing, of course, a $\frac{1}{4}$" hole or slot to take the tripod screw is drilled through the base plate. Small end stops from $\frac{1}{4}$" perspex may be cemented to front or rear of base, plate to prevent the camera from swivelling when clamped in position.

57

Method 2. This method may be more convenient for some of the high and narrow cine cameras which do not give sufficient clearance between cylinder wall and fixed base plate for a tripod screw. An acrylic gland installed internally or externally may be used in conjunction with a hold down bolt suitably cut to length. Alternatively a 'flat' can be filed on the internal wall of the cylinder and the washer provided with will then form an effective seal when screwed up tight against the cylinder wall. An upper support cradle may be installed if desired by cementing $\frac{1}{4}''$ flat perspex as indicated.

Method 3. To avoid piercing the tubing this method may be used. Two upper fixed rails are cemented to the inside walls of the tube and the camera bolted to a lower bevelled piece of perspex slides into position below the fixed rails. This method is rather more tricky than methods 1 and 2 and care must be taken to fix the upper rails accurately to provide a smooth fit for the lower base plate.

To sum up basically any method which rigidly fixes the camera inside the housing and allows it to be removed quickly and easily is O.K. (but avoid attaching camera to front or rear faces). Other methods will suggest themselves according to individual requirements.

TAKE CARE: Avoid the impulse to rush ahead and get the housing completed in record time. A little extra care and thought in the early stages, will be rewarded later by a really professional housing, which you will be proud to use and display.

FITTING OF CONTROLS AND GLANDS: Having secured the camera firmly in position the next job is to fit the lever wind control. This is generally the most tricky one to fit and you should consider the situation carefully before going ahead. The shaft must obviously line up with the centre of the lever, knob or crank on the camera and consequently there is no choice regarding the position for installation of the gland. First mark the location on the outside cylinder wall using a chinagraph or grease pencil. To determine the position use a straight edge or drawing set triangle and with the camera in position sight from various angles and mark where a line perpendicular to the camera body would intersect the outer cylinder wall and the centre of the wind knob on the camera.

HYDROSEAL glands have been specially developed for use on curved surfaces. A 1″ diameter provides ample cementing surface for support of the shaft and an 'O' ring fitted in the gland allows a push pull action which is often required.

Much testing has been done by Aquamatic and the Single Cruciform Section 'O' ring has proved to be perfectly adequate for all depths normally obtained. This type of ring is a special feature of all our glands and in

58

effect provides two sealing edges on one 'O' ring, with really smooth operation. This method is in fact capable of withstanding a thousand or so p.s.i. with the precision ground stainless steel shaft, and there is a considerable safety margin while operating at a maximum of the 100 or so p.s.i. to which skin divers operate.

The 'O' ring is fitted towards one end of the gland, thus permitting the other end to be cut at an angle and shaped to fit a curved surface. It may be installed inside or outside as the seal resists pressure from either direction. Study figures 1 to 6 which describe methods of mounting.

Meanwhile you are ready to drill the first hole. The secret is sharp tools and correct procedure. Holes should be drilled with metal cutting twist drills using light pressure and slow cutting speeds. A drill press is very useful for this purpose. Make sure that the job is rigidly held or clamped in position and lift the drill from hole frequently to remove shavings and prevent excess heat build up. The tool or drill should be ground to a zero rake angle to prevent grabbing or chattering.

Thus using a $\frac{1}{4}$" drill, make the hole through the cylinder wall and once through rotate drill slightly to provide clearance for the shaft.

Slip a shaft into position and check for clearance and alignment. The hole should clear the shaft completely which should line up precisely with the centre of the camera control. If necessary ream out using a rats tail file. Lubricate the shaft and inside bore of the gland with vasoline or silicon grease, slide gland into position and mark approximate angle and position for cutting. First make a rough cut with hacksaw or band saw and try again to fit. Trim with a disc, drum sander or file and work down gradually until the shaft lines up perfectly when the gland is held TIGHT against the wall. A useful tip in getting the curvature correct is to tape a piece of sand paper to the cylinder (with a piece of thin cardboard beneath to prevent scratching) either inside or outside as necessary, and then slide gland backwards and forwards to work down to correct curvature. This sounds an irksome task but is in fact quite easy and only takes a few minutes. If you object to using the expensive tubing for this operation a saucepan or similar item of approximately the same diameter as the tube is ideal.

Having got the angle to your satisfaction champher the edge of the hole slightly by hand using a $\frac{3}{8}$" or $\frac{1}{2}$" drill to provide a well for excess cement.

Make sure that the hole is free from chips of perspex and surfaces to be cemented are clean and grease free.

Prop the cylinder in position such that the area to be cemented is horizontal. Coat the stainless steel shaft lightly with grease and insert in the gland. Cover the surface of the gland with an even coat of Tensol 7 (prepared by mixing components A to B in proportions 25:1 in a test tube or on a piece of aluminium foil). With the camera in position insert the shaft and gland and check alignment, rotate slightly if necessary and squeeze out bubbles by applying light pressure. Allow the gland at least 3 hours to set and then remove the shaft. Leave overnight before attempting any further operations on this area.

The method described above applies to fitting of any gland either on flat or curved surfaces.

Warnings
1. Any knob or other device secured to a shaft requires a flat, ground or filed and any sharp edges removed by use of emery paper or a grinding wheel.
2. Any burr on the precision ground shaft will tear the 'O' ring as it is drawn through the gland and render it useless. Also if the shaft is cut then the end MUST be bevelled and smoothed similar to the original shaft ends.
3. Do not attempt to use a shaft not provided with the gland—even a small variation in diameter and surface finish could cause problems.
4. If the shaft tends to bind due to misalignment or cement in hole, a tightly rolled piece of emery or twist drill PARTLY inserted will ease the fit. DO NOT attempt to ream out the bore of the gland itself or sand the 'O' ring. Fitting of other controls will be more simple and they should be positioned for convenience of operation.

The next job is to fit the stud retainers for clamping the rear plate in position. This is easily achieved using small G clamps. Work the stud retainers to the correct curvature by sanding as previously explained and cement in position using Tensol 7 from flat stock. Drill holes in backplate after cementing retainers and exact position can be determined.

Front Plate
Finally the front plate is cemented in position. Remove controls to ease this all important operation. Select a piece of scratch free paper covered perspex and cut to external diameter of cylinder. Stand the tube on a couple of books or blocks. Cover inner and outer walls below joint with masking tape, ensure that the tube is clean and grease free and give a generous coat of Tensol 7. Lower the disc carefully in position and place 10 to 15 pounds weight on top. Cement will be squeezed out around the edges providing a clear joint. A few isolated bubbles are quite acceptable and will not affect the strength and watertightness of the joint.

Leave overnight for joint to cure, remove the masking tape and finally sand and polish the edge of the disc, to provide a neat finish.

Watertightness—Methods of Checking
1. A simple test is to fill the case with warm soapy water, if none leaks out you are reasonably sure that joints are watertight.
2. An alternative method is to install a pressurising valve, then with the housing completely assembled a couple of strokes with a hand pump will increase the internal pressure and on immersion of the housing a stream of bubbles will indicate any leaks.

60

Warning

Pressurising is not recommended for normal use of the housing as the rear plate seal is designed for external pressures. Also there is a danger that multi-element lenses may be damaged due to unequal pressures on the components of the system. There have been various cases of housings blowing up due to over pressurising. A few strokes only is necessary for testing purposes.

Another method is to tie the housing in a sheet weighted with lead and lower for 5–10 mins. to about 20 ft. in the sea. If there is any water found inside then the point of failure will be noticed by a streak of droplets, on the inner walls of the enclosure.

If all is well and you are happy that the case is watertight, install the camera and check for buoyancy.

Ballasting

Views on buoyancy vary but in general approximately neutral should be aimed at and the individual can trim to his own requirements.

Fixing handles to your enclosure. $1\frac{1}{4}''$ diameter hollow PVC tubes are attached to the housing by $\frac{3}{8}''$ or $\frac{1}{2}''$ perspex blocks cemented to the outside wall of the tubing as indicated. Ballast is then provided by filling the tubes with lead to give the required buoyancy. A couple of holes in the upper support bracket can be provided for a neck lanyard if required.

To what depth will the housing be safe?

Aquamatic have standardised on $\frac{3}{8}''$ wall thickness which is ideal from strength, economy and weight considerations. It provides adequate wall thickness for turning the 'O' ring groove without leaving a thin fragile wall. End plates tend to 'dish' under pressure and as a general rule, $\frac{3}{8}''$ end plates are suitable for up to 6" tube diameter for a safe working depth of 150'. 6", 7" and 8" tubes with $\frac{3}{8}''$ plates are O.K. to 100'. Above 100' use $\frac{1}{2}''$ especially with 8" or larger tubing. If you intend to use the housing at extreme depths over 200'—then use $\frac{3}{4}''$ thick.

Note: End plates should be of equal thickness since the strength will be determined by the thinner of the two.

Cruciform 'O' ring seal glands if installed correctly as per instructions will withstand pressures in excess of 300'.

Camera Handling

Never handle the camera with wet hands or when wearing a wet suit which can act as a trap for stray water. Make sure that no sand or grit has become trapped under the 'O' rings as this can make them leak and flood the case. Grease 'O' rings with special silicone lubricant at regular intervals to keep them supple and always take a supply of spare 'O' rings on a trip away from base. Be especially careful of camera cases when leaving the water, particularly when crawling out of the foam onto a rocky beach. They can all too easily swing and come crashing down against some jagged rocks. If they do not shatter they are likely to get scratched badly. Do not leave the case in direct sunlight. It does not do it any good and may bring you misting problems when you dive.

Housing Care
Housing must be well washed in fresh water after use to remove all traces of salt. Perspex surfaces should be regularly washed with an antistatic compound and brass sections kept polished. Scratches can be removed using the polishes listed below.

Polish No. 1—Coarse for deep scratches.
Polish No. 2a—Fine for light scratches and finishing.
Polish No. 3—Antistatic compound. Neutralises effect and restores lustre.

Supplier: Aquamatic, 40 Benslow Rise, Hitchin, Herts.

Cine-Photography
The same technical problems apply, but the film cameraman has a slightly easier task as he can pan his camera to cover a wide area.

When making an underwater movie make sure something interesting is happening, in each shot as moving films require *movement* to keep the audience interested. Change camera to subject distances and angles to provide additional interest. For example, start with a medium long shot which locates the divers, say approaching a wreck. Now come in for a close up of the diver examining part of the wreck. Perhaps shoot through a porthole or frame the approach of the divers in a weed fringed doorway.

When panning the camera move it very slowly and smoothly or the result will be unsatisfactory. Try a couple of rehearsal pans so that you can see exactly where you will start and stop.

Zooming into a subject is easy, all you have to do is fin gently towards it. Zooming out is more difficult because your fins are likely to kick up sediment which will spoil the picture. If you intend to edit the film afterwards make sure you give yourself plenty of cut-away shots. These are brief sequences which are used to break up longer scenes. Examples of the cut-away technique can be seen during television news interviews. The camera will suddenly cut to the reporter for a few seconds and then back to the subject. In this way any stops and starts in filming and interviewing can be disguised.

If your camera has variable frame speeds shoot some footage at high speed, to give a slow motion effect on the screen. This can produce a very attractive sequence, especially if combined with a finning zoom towards the subject. When finning, with or without slow motion camera techniques, make sure your progress through the water is slow and steady to prevent a jerky sequence.

It is best to prepare some sort of script when shooting movie film, even

62

if this is no more than a few jotted notes or a mental outline of the shots you require. A typical shooting script might look like this.

1. Medium close-up (m.c.u.) of divers kitting up aboard diving boat.
2. Cut-away close-up (c.u.) of different pieces of equipment being fitted. This will enable you to edit from partially kitted to fully kitted up divers without a jerk in the time sequence of film.
3. Divers going backwards out of boat (m.c.u.)
4. Underwater shot of divers entering water, medium long shot (m.l.s.)
5. Finning down after divers (m.l.s.)
6. Close-up of diver checking compass (cut-away) (c.u.)
7. Medium shot of divers approaching sea bed (m.l.s.)
8. Shot of diver pointing (m.c.u.)
9. Shot of divers swimming towards wreck (m.l.s.)
10. From wreck, shot of divers approaching (m.l.s.)
11. Shot of diver rubbing off weed and crustacean (m.c.u.)
12. Shot of divers reading name of wreck (m.c.u.)

Exposures for movie making are made as in stills work. If the light level is too low then movie lights can be used to illuminate the scene, but remember that, as with flash, they can only cover a limited area.

In General
Compared with the miles of film exposed on land each year the number of underwater pictures taken is negligible. There is great scope for experimentation with equipment and treatment of subjects. Always take more pictures below the surface than you would above it. If an interesting subject swims into view then fire off as many frames as possible, changing angle, distance and exposure settings to get as wide a range of effects as possible.

6

Advanced Techniques

Most cameras used underwater take their pictures through a flat glass port. This results in the problems detailed in the last chapter, which can be summarised as follows.

Due to the effects of refraction the subject appears one third larger because both the photographer and the camera lens are viewing an apparent image of the subject at $\frac{3}{4}$ of its true distance. The angle of coverage of the lens is reduced to about $\frac{3}{4}$ of its coverage in air. Both these effects mitigate against the photographer who must work as close as possible to his subject to overcome the problems of light absorption and scatter. In addition, lenses operating through flat ports lose image quality because of a number of optical aberrations. There is loss of image definition, especially towards the edge of the frame due to chromatic aberrations. These are particularly apparent when using the very wide angle lens necessary in a flat port case. Apart from chromatic aberrations there is likely to be pin-cushion distortion of the image caused by the magnification of the outer edges of the picture being greater than the central portions. However, this only becomes a serious problem whin trying to accurately record objects which have straight edges and square corners.

All these difficulties can be overcome by using a dome port in place of the flat port window. In the past dome ports were difficult to construct and costly to buy, as they had to be blown from glass. It is now possible to mould nearly optically perfect domes out of perspex. These are cheap and can easily be replaced if they become too scratched for use, always a hazard with perspex, although with a dome port they have to be very badly marked indeed to seriously affect the image quality as the sea water tends to fill in and reduces abrasions.

A pioneer in the design dome-ports and one of the foremost experts in their use is the American photographer Flip Schulke to whom I am indebted for the information on their optical properties and the problems which have to be overcome in using them successfully.

In order to gain the full correction that the dome port affords, the in-air lens and the dome must be mounted so that the centre of the lens and the centre of curvature of the dome coincide. When that happens the light rays passing through the port and lens do so at right angles without being refracted and so the in-air coverage angle of the lens is maintained. A 20 mm lens behind a flat port has an effective focal length nearer 30 mm. When used with a dome port the focal length and angle of coverage are preserved.

The first sea dive, a student skin-diver gets sea bed instruction in shallow water during his first descent. (See chapter four)

Wreck hunters explore a modern wreck sixty feet down in the North Sea. The remains of the funnel and superstructure lie across the sea bed. (See chapter four)

A diver returns to the surface after diving in the Indian Ocean. (See chapter four)

With practice you can explore a great deal of coast on a snorkel dive. (See chapter four)

In water the dome port becomes a strong negative lens which reduces the apparent object/lens distance even more than when using a flat port. For example if you are using a dome port of $4\frac{1}{3}''$ radius to photograph an object 8 ft. distance the apparent image seen by the lens will be only 15.6 in away. In other words you will be taking a close-up picture of the distant object. The degree of magnification varies according to the radius of curvature of the dome in use. Smaller domes produce the greatest reduction in apparent distance.

Close-up photography requires either an extension tube to move the lens further away from the film plane or the use of a close-up lens. The following table gives an example of the close-up lenses needed with different dome-ports.

Radius of curvature of dome-port	Close-up lens
3.5 in (89 mm)	+5
6 in (152 mm)	+3
8 in (203 mm)	None provided the lens can focus down to 2 ft (610)

1 A dome-port therefore affects the accuracy of the focus scale which may no longer be used until it has been recalibrated either by calculations or trial and error. If you are using reflex focusing then no adjustments are necessary.

Although the dome-port makes the footage scale even more inaccurate than the flat-port it does provide good correction of the underwater magnification effect. The object is seen by the system not only at a much shorter apparent object distance but also at a proportionally smaller size. As the object distance shrinks the apparent object distance shrinks in exactly the same proportion. The camera sees a nearer object of a smaller size, and one effect compensates for the other to keep the angular dimensions constant. Not only is the objectives in-air coverage angle maintained by the dome-port systems but also nothing is lost of the object. There is no cropping, and the object is reproduced on the same scale as it would be reproduced by the same lens at the same real distance with in-air photography.

According to Flip Schulke other abberrations caused by refraction are also corrected to a great extent by the dome-port system. Dome-ports can also be used with the Nikonos and Calypsophot cameras providing the underwater photographer with an extremely versatile and easily transported system. An ideal lens for use with the dome-port is the old 21 mm Nikon, now out of production, which may be picked up secondhand for a modest sum. This lens had the disadvantage from a surface photographers point-of-view, of requiring a separate finder, because its long barrel meant that the reflex camera's mirror had to be locked up out of the way. However, this is quite unimportant to the underwater photographer using a Nikonos. Fish-eye lenses can also be used with dome-ports. These provide a 360° circular picture. To my mind this is quite a pleasing effect when used in moderation but gets extremely tedious after a short time. I would therefore be more inclined to recommend the 21 mm lens as the ideal partner for dome-ports.

Before leaving sophisticated underwater lens systems, mention should be made of the water contact lenses now being produced. Unlike the dome port system, which can be used on land under adverse weather conditions provided the close-up lens is removed, the water contact lenses cannot be used on the surface as the front element is computed to work in direct contact with water. These lenses have been pioneered by Nikon Optical of Japan and cost several hundreds of pounds. They have so far designed and marketed a corrected 28 mm lens and a fully corrected 15 mm lens for use with their Nikonos cameras. The focal lengths are given as in-air focal lengths, even though the lenses can only be used underwater. In effect, therefore, the 28 mm lens gives the same angle of coverage underwater as a 35 mm lens, while the 15 mm lens is the equivalent to a 20 mm lens in-air. These are extremely ingenious pieces of equipment but I have some doubt that all the design faults have been overcome. Flip showed me a 15 mm lens bought in America with some pride, but only a few weeks later wrote to say that it had flooded, something which has never happened with his dome-ports.

Flash

Except where some types of scientific record shot are required, most underwater photographers want to obtain pictures which look as natural as possible. For this reason some dislike using flash which can cause harsh foreground contrasts and completely black backgrounds. When using a small flash source close to the lens this flat, unreal lighting is inevitable. One answer is to more the flash away from the lens axis on a long arm which directs the light in at about 45° to the subject producing a better modelling effect. Underwater this directional lighting must be handled with care as strong side-lighting looks completely unnatural.

A different solution is to use a small flash source not as the main source of illumination but simply to fill-in the details of the subject. With a focal plane shutter, use long burning focal plane bulbs. If you fill-in with electronic flash the slow shutter speed (about 1/60th) required for synchronisation may mean that two images of rapidly moving objects are recorded. One, sharp, by flash and the other, slightly blurred, by available light. A between-the-lens shutter, such as is fitted to the Rolleiflex, enables electronic flash to be synchronised at any shutter speed and so this source can be satisfactorily used as a fill-in.

A more involved technique is to use two flash sources, one at the camera position, to provide the fill-in, and the main modelling lamp, in a separate underwater housing, at some distance away. It will have to be held and positioned by a diver assistant who is familiar with the principles of photographic lighting and care must be taken that the synchronising lead doesn't come into picture. Alternatively the main light can be triggered using a photo-electric slave which will trigger it in response to light from the fill-in lamp. In use care must be taken to ensure that the photo-cell trigger is of a sufficiently wide angle and correctly positioned to pick up the flash signal.

Calculating exposures when using two flash heads is no more complicated than using a single source providing that your fill-in light is correctly adjusted so that it is not putting out too much light. Calculate on the basis of the distance between the main light and the subject, although here again experience and practice are a better guide than any theoretical formula.

If the camera mounted flash synchronises by means of a direct lead from gun to camera, then there is a risk of electric shock if the housing floods. To prevent this, and to enable the flash to be unplugged underwater, an intermediate relay switch may be used. You can construct such a system quite simply from an old capacitator bulb gun. From the original flash bulb contacts you run two wires to a small relay switch. The electronic flash gun co-axial contacts are joined to the other relay terminals so that when the relay closes, the gun fires. The synchronisation contacts from the old capacitor gun are soldered onto a co-axial socket mounted in the flash housing. It is into this socket that the synchronisation lead from the camera plugs. When the shutter fires the relay is triggered via a 22 volt battery and the capacitor. In this way only a low, safe voltage ever passes through the camera system.

Focus Problems

Focusing a camera, even a reflex camera in dim light, can be quite a problem. In *Fish Watching and Photography*, a book which I would commend to all interested in marine life and photography, the authors report on an ingenious focusing system developed by Geoff Harwood. This is a sub-aqua adaptation of a device used by American newspaper photographers several years ago when the large format press cameras were still in use. These cameras focused by means of a long-base range finder. For night-time work a powerful light source was designed which screwed into the top of the range-finder and projected two thin beams of light onto the subject. As the focus was adjusted the beams converged and, when they met, the cameraman knew that his picture was sharp. This is approximately the system which Geoff Harwood has perfected for dim light underwater photography. He mounts one pencil torch inside his camera housing, a second on a sliding scale in the perspex flash-housing. By adjusting the angle of the torch in his flash housing, against a calibrated scale he can "set" the light rays to converge at the required distance.

To photograph a fish lurking in some dark rock cave he simply sets the scale and then fins in, watching the two dots of light on the focusing screen of his reflex camera. When the light dots slide into a single spot he fires the shutter. Using electronic flash, which is necessary anyhow when working in the dim conditions for which this aid was developed, the focusing spot is washed out by the much more powerful source. The system provides a remarkably simple and reliable technique for overcoming a major underwater difficulty.

Close-up

Close-up lenses are available as accessories for the Nikonos in the SOS range in England and Hydro Photo in America. If you use an in-air camera in an underwater housing it is perfectly possible to fit on an ordinary close-up lens before diving, although this will limit your camera to shooting close-ups for the duration of that dive. Some divers achieve excellent results merely by fixing magnifying lenses in front of their camera housing ports. These systems have to be calibrated by trial and error.

It is easier when working with a non-reflex camera to use some type of close-up frame so that your lens is always at the correct distance from the subject. This focusing aid need be no more than a length of brass or stainless steel rod bent into the correct image area. This camera-frame distance can be worked out using a ruler, your underwater camera and a tub full of water in the bathroom. The frame is then mounted on rods at the correct distance from the camera for the close-up lens in use. Needless to say a focusing frame is only useful for static marine life, sea urchins, anemones and so on, it can hardly be used for taking pictures of fast moving fish!

Colour Correction Filters

These can be bought cheaply in the form of gelatine sheets and then cut for use. With an in-air camera they can be fitted in front of the lens using a mount with two optical flats of glass to hold them in place. Great care must be taken when handling these gels as grease from fingerprints, dust or dirt will reduce image definition. If you are using a Nikonos or Calypsophot the gels can be mounted inside the camera over the rear element of the lens with a few specks of silicone grease.

Too much blue in the water can be corrected by using a red filter, too much green by means of magenta filter. In blue or blue green water down to ten to fifteen feet use a Kodak *CCR 20* filter, at depths between 20 and 40 feet use a Kodak *CCR 40*. Below this depth electronic or bulb flash will probably be necessary anyhow. In green northern waters a light magenta filter, the Kodak *CCM 30* can be used, but great care must be taken not to over-filter with magenta.

Filters must be treated with respect. Gelatine sheets are badly affected by moisture and shouldn't be handled with even damp fingers. If even slightly damaged or soiled they should be discarded.

Ultra-voilet filters have no application underwater, but it is perhaps worth mentioning that they will give lenses good protection from spray if land cameras are being used to take shots in the diving boat or on the harbour side prior to a dive. UV filters require no exposure correction but the others discussed will require increased exposure to compensate for the light they absorb. Mount a strip of the same filter in front of the exposure meter photo-cell. Now use the meter in the normal way and set the camera according to the reading it gives.

Flooded Camera
Even the best made perspex cases and the most expensive commercial housings can flood. If they do then your camera may still be saved provided you take prompt and intelligent action.

The first essential is to keep the camera underwater and out of the air. Leave it in the flooded case until you can get to a source of fresh water. Then place the camera in a container and flood it with fresh water. Try to keep as much air out of the water as possible, one way is to use a hose to gently fill the container. Leave it in running fresh water for up to twenty minutes, continually working the controls. When well washed out the camera must be taken home in a container of fresh water.

From tap water transfer it to a bath of boiled or distilled water, still working all the controls at regular intervals, winding on and firing the shutter, changing the shutter speed and f-stops. Then dry out the camera using a bath of methylated spirits.

Remove the leather trim to get at the screws and strip down the camera using instrument makers screwdrivers. Take as many of the assemblies as possible apart. It may be helpful to the mechanic who has to put it all together again if you keep various assemblies separated in small containers. The cogs, gears, linkages, screws and springs should now be dropped into brake fluid and left there until they can be transported to a mechanic. The lens itself should on no account be placed in brake fluid but simply dried out after the meths treatment.

Some parts of the camera will be ruined by the rescue treatment. Shutter blinds, plastic focusing screens, will have to be replaced but the cost of the damage will still have been reduced to the lowest possible sum. Without this treatment, and if you allow the camera to dry out with salt water inside its insides then you can write it off completely. Flooded cameras happen to the most professional underwater photographers. Peter Scoones, one of Britain's best known underwater photographers, has drowned and saved his cameras on a number of occasions. He can strip down and reassemble a Bronica or Bolex with equal apparent ease and aplomb. But unless you have his experience look in the Yellow Pages or ask your local dealer for the name of a mechanic experienced with your type of camera.

Manufacturers and suppliers of advanced underwater equipment:
Flip Sckulke Enterprises. Can supply dome-port housings for range of lenses, 21 mm and fish-eye. European Sales Manager David Benda, 125 Fennells, Harlow, Essex.

American address: P.O. Box 430760 Miami, Florida, 33143. U.S.A.

Interspace Design Systems Ltd. Middle Street, Shere, Surrey. Phone: Shere 2252. Produce underwater electronic flash units from the basic to the extremely sophisticated and can also make up cases for standard surface guns.

Those interested in underwater photography as a hobby in itself should consider joining the British Society of Underwater Photographers. Formed in 1967 by underwater cameramen who realised the need to organise and co-ordinate their work the membership is world-wide. It enables underwater photographers, experts and beginners alike to exchange information and ideas. There are regular monthly meetings which include basic instruction for beginners, discussions about the latest technical innovations and developments. Members also get a valuable data book which includes technical and general information as well as an extremely valuable guide suppliers of unusual photographic accessories. The society has weekend dives and started a picture agency Seaphot especially to sell members work to the increasing number of markets—everything from magazine publishers to jig-saw makers —available.

Useful Books:
In Water Photography. L. E. Martens, John Wiley and Sons, London.
Camera Underwater. H. E. Dobbs, Focal Press, London, 1962
Underwater Photography. Schneck and Kendall. Cornell Maritime Press, Cambridge, Maryland, U.S.A.
The Art of Underwater Photographt. Stark and Brundza, Amphoto, New York
Guide to Underwater Photography. Rebikoff and Cherney, Chilton, U.S.A., 1965
Fish Watching and Photography. Kendall McDonald with others. John Murray. London, 1972. (See Chapter Nine book list for full desription of this valuable manual).

7

Wreck Hunting

Divers hunt wrecks for many reasons, most of them good, a few of them sad, bad and illegal. It may be the thrill of scientific discovery on an archaeological expedition, or the hope of legitimate salvage on a wreck which you have bought, it may be no more than the excitement of exploration. Hopefully it will not be in search of plunder which not only puts the diver on the wrong side of the law and helps to give the sport a bad name, but may lead to the total destruction of a valuable archaeological site.

Wrecks which are more than a hundred years old on the day of their discovery are said to be historic sites and may qualify for legal protection if they have any particular interest or merit. Even if they are fairly modern wrecks removing any object from them is against the law unless the correct procedures are followed. I will deal with the legal aspect of wreck hunting in a moment.

After being on the bottom for only a few years, many wrecks bear little resemblance to the vessels they were on the day of launch. Hulls collapse, steel plates become encrusted with marine life, even large items of machinery such as winches and boilers, can soon become so smothered in weed and crustaceans that only their artificially straight outlines will distinguish them from the rocks and boulders amongst which they lie. Wooden wrecks on sand may soon vanish completely under the shifting seabed with only a few fragments of metal, cannons perhaps or an anchor, to mark their final resting place deep beneath the ocean floor.

In this chapter I want to consider rather more substantial wrecks, modern steel vessels for the most part, whose outlines are still ship like and whose value lies in salvage or providing an exciting dive. Wreck hunting, like most good detective stories, usually begins with the discovery of the body in the shape of some mysterious vessel not apparently marked on any Admiralty chart. Despite the care with which wrecks are plotted, in order to keep the seaways safe for other vessels, there is a vast number of vessels ranging from small trawlers and first world war transports, to downed World War II aircraft, cargo vessels, and yachts, whose identity has been lost in the course of time.

If you do come across a large, unchartered wreck finding out who owns her can become more than just a matter of satisfying your idle curiosity. The vessel may be extremely valuable from a salvage point-of-view and it is only by tracing her identity and locating the owners, that you can make a bid for the wreck in order to commence legal salvage operations. Even if curiosity is your only motive, tracking down the history of a wreck you have discovered makes a fascinating exercise with which to while away the winter. From a starting point of a few scraps of marine encrusted metal it is often possible to build up a complete picture of the vessel of which they once formed a part, know why she sank and where she was launched, what cargo she carried and if there was any drama surrounding her loss.

An excellent example of the way in which such detective work can be carried out is given by Kendall McDonald in his book *The Wreck Detectives*. In May, 1966 a team of divers from the Kingston Branch of the British Sub Aqua Club were trailing their anchors across the seabed at Swanage Bay, Dorset in the hope of latching onto some interesting obstruction. When they did, one anchor caught such a firm bite that the line parted! However the anchor on the second diving boat also snagged the obstruction and held firm. Divers went down and found themselves standing on the deck of a magnificent wreck whose vast expanses of teak deck vanished into the gloom on either side of the rail where they had touched down. This was a very wreck like wreck, with glass still in the portholes, a massive winch in position on the upper deck and wireless insulators on the mast. These indicated that she was probably an early 20th century vessel . . . but what craft was she?

The first clue was provided in a letter from the Admiralty's Hydrographic Department. The nearest charted wreck, they said, was a 6953 ton Australian owned vessel, the *Kyarra*, which had been sunk by a German U-boat in 1918. Local gossip which spoke of a hospital ship being torpedoed in Swanage Bay during the last year of the war also seemed to tie in with the wreck they had found. The problem was the chart position of the *Kyarra* and the ship they had located was different.

Working on the basis that she might be the *Kyarra*, wrongly charted, the Kingston divers explored the wreck for more clues. The discovery of some sealing wax with a Sydney manufacturers name still clearly embossed on it seemed to confirm that the wreck was the *Kyarra* and the Admiralty position was in error.

Meanwhile the Branch had written to *Lloyds Register of Shipping* for further information and were told the date of the *Kyarra's* construction, 1903, and the name of the shipbuilders, Messrs. W. Denny and Brothers of Dumbarton. Lloyds of London were able to add that the *Kyarra*, had been sunk on May 26th during a voyage from London to Sydney.

From their records the Imperial War Museum supplied detailed information about the vessel's construction. The *Kyarra* had had two decks, one of steel *sheathed in teak*. She had electric light and wireless and was described as a twin-screwed schooner. Her skipper had been a W. Smith and six of the crew had died during the submarine attack. The War Museum added that the *Kyarra* had been a hospital ship and had taken part in landing Anzac troops at the Dardenelles.

W. Denny and Brothers of Dumbarton were no longer in business, but the National Maritime Museum at Greenwich housed the bulk of their building records. The *Kyarra* was launched in February, 1903 and had two masts on which she could, in an emergency, set sail. Her main motive power was provided by two triple expansion engines of 375 Nominal Horse Power. She had 42 first class cabins with 3 berths in each and 20 second class cabins with 8 berths, the lower decks had been fitted out as cattle stalls. The Maritime Museum added that they had plans of the ship in their library, copies of which could be provided if needed.

The original owners, the Australasia United Steam Ship Company, whose name had been supplied by Lloyds Register of Shipping, had also gone out of business, but much patient letter writing revealed that the company had been taken over by another shipping firm, Inchcape and Company. They were as helpful as the rest of the organisations involved and, from their records, were able to complete the story of the *Kyarra* up to the moment when she left on her final, fateful voyage. Fitted out as a hospital ship during the winter of 1917, she sailed from Tilbury on May 24th en route to Devonport where she was to embark a thousand sick and wounded Australian troops bound for Sydney. This voyage was brutally terminated by the German U-boat.

As a result of the discovery of the wreck being publicised, an eye-witness to the actual sinking came forward and told her story to the local paper. "With horror we saw her sinking rapidly by the bow. She was so close (to shore) that we could see the launching of her lifeboat and after about only seven minutes the stern seemed to rear up as she plunged below the surface.

"We wept as we thought of the wounded trapped in her ... It was believed that the offending German submarine was the one which was cornered and sunk near Sandbanks shortly afterwards."

The vessel was finally and unquestionably confirmed as the *Kyarra* when the Kingston divers located her bell and brought it to the surface. The War Damage Commission who had paid the original owners £190,000 for her loss, were willing to sell and for a mere £120 the Branch acquired the magnificent wreck.

The story of the *Kyarra* is interesting because it shows just how much information can be gleaned by patient detective work and knowing where to ask. When tracking down a wreck's history, therefore, you should make use of some, or all, of the sources listed below.

1) *Local gossip*

This may not be very accurate in the finer details, but it can provide vital clues which just aren't forthcoming from any other source. Coastguards, present and past, fishermen and local boatmen, harbour officials and lifeboat men call all help you track down the identity of a wreck. Local newspaper records, often kept in the reference department of the nearest major library, are also valuable in supplying dates and eye-witness accounts. Where older wrecks are concerned histories of the area and old guide books may provide a clue.

2) *The Wrecks Section*: Hydrographic Department, Ministry of Defence, Beadon Road, Taunton, Somerset.
In 1913 this government department began a card index system of all potential shipping hazards. Their records hold details of all known wrecks from this year onwards and they can provide information about the name of the vessel, the tonnage, the date it was sunk and how much water lies over the wreck. A fee is charged for making the search, how much will depend on the time it takes. To be able to help they need to know either the latitude and longtitude of the wreck of a distinctive landmark by which to identify it. For example three miles due south of Beachy Head lighthouse.

Lloyd's Register of Shipping: 69–71 Fenchurch Street, London EC3 M4BS.
Given the name of the vessel and date of loss they can provide a brief history of the wreck and how she sank.

Imperial War Museum: Lambeth Road, London SE1 6HZ.
They can only provide information about British merchant ships and Royal Navy vessels lost in action during the two World Wars. Ships lost during this same period by storm or other natural disaster are not listed.

Lloyd's: Lime Stree, London, EC3M 7HA.
For a search fee, how much depends on the time required to find the information, they can provide details about the way the vessel was lost, the cargo she carried and the ownership at the time of loss. Lloyd's records are world wide.

The National Maritime Museum, Greenwich, London SE10 9NF.
They have a first class library with all the main shipping registers and lists, plus hundreds of books, articles and reports on different shipwrecks. They also have a superb picture library of every type of illustration ranging from oils to photographs. Copies can be obtained at a reasonable price.

Air Historical Branch: RAF, Queen Anne's Chambers, 3 Dean Farrar Street, London SW1H 9JX.
Although seldom of any salvage value you may want to know more about the section of Lancaster or Spitfire which you fish out of the deep. So many aircraft crashed off the South Coast during the last war that

most divers will come across at least one aerial wreck. If you have the aircraft's number the Historical Branch of the RAF will be able to fill in details of the unit, squadron and pilot's name.

Flight Safety Branch FS3b: RAF, Tavistock House, 1–6 Tavistock Square, London WC1H 9NL.
If you locate an aircraft the local newspapers may have details about the type of machine involved and the date it came down. Armed with these facts you may be able to get further information from the above address.

Salvage and the Law

Maritime law is extremely complex, but you must start from the assumption that somebody, somewhere owns the wreck which you have found. Even if they don't you cannot just tear it apart. Under the Merchant Shipping Act of 1894 any matter relating to wrecks is the responsibility of the Receiver of Wrecks who is an official of the Department of Trade and Industry. He has wide powers, including a right to arrest anybody found plundering or interfering with a wreck.

If you discover a wreck which does not appear on the latest Admiralty chart your first task is to report the find to the Receiver of Wrecks. If you salvage any materials without owning the wreck you will have broken no law provided you hand over all your trophies to the Receiver as soon as possible. Material which is sold off by the Receiver benefits the divers who found it, in some circumstances they may now get the whole net proceeds of the sale.

There is nothing to stop you keeping all the salvage value providing you can trace the owner of the wreck, often the Insurance Company which paid out for its loss, and buy the wreck from them. How much the wreck will cost depends on its value as scrap, any cargo it may contain and how difficult a salvage operation is likely to prove. Kingston Branch, as we have seen, bought a wreck which had cost the War Damage Commission nearly £200,000 for a mere £120. An American salvage expert did even better, some might think, when he picked up the *Lusitania* for £1,000. The salvage value of this luxury liner, which was sunk by a German torpedo off the Irish coast during the First War and now lies at a depth of some 300 ft. runs into millions. The snag is that most experts regard any major salvage operation as next to impossible.

Wreck Location

If you find an uncharted wreck the first job is to take accurate bearings so that you can dive again on exactly the right spot. Mark the site with a suitable buoy, if possible, but use an inflatable plastic buoy which will not damage any small craft that happens to run into it. Use wire and not rope attaching the wire to a high point on the wreck and giving it extra

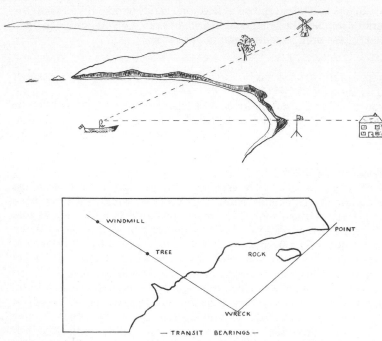

Fig. 3. Taking a transit bearing by lining up two sets of objects on shore.

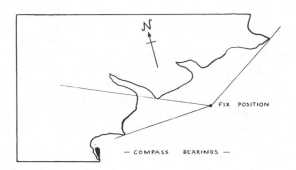

Fig. 4. Transit Bearing. Line up two sets of on shore objects to mark a spot at sea.
To fix a position using the compass take three bearings from on shore objects.

support by using a small, non-collapsible buoy fixed below the surface—at all states of the tide—to ensure that the cable remains taut. Even when you are able to buoy the wreck in this way it is still important to take bearings so that you can return to the wire without wasting time.

76

The simplest way to fix your position at sea is by means of two sets of marks on land. For example, a tall building which lines up with a tree as one mark and, perhaps, a harbour jetty lighthouse which lines up with a line of cliffs for the other. When all these marks are in the right relationship your boat will be back on site.

It is often valuable to take photographs from the boat in order to assist with the site location. There are, of course, more scientific methods of fixing your position, with a compass or with a sextant. Of the two, the compass method is definitely less accurate. Sextants, which are now made in plastic and can be bought quite cheaply and mastered without much difficulty, measure angles horizontally or vertically. For wreck location they are mainly used in the horizontal mode. Two angles between two charted marks are measured and then transferred to a chart, either by drawing them out, using a protractor, on tracing paper and then laying them down on the chart, or by using an instrument known as a Station Pointer. This consists of a protractor with one fixed and two moveable arms. The fixed arm is lined up with the central bearing and the other arms moved to the angles which co-incide with your compass bearing.

If there is a wreck in a particular area you will probably learn of it first from the local fisherman who get their nets snagged up. Trawlermen keep record of such troublesome locations and may prove extremely informative for the price of a pint.

Once you have located a general area you can pin-point the vessel either electronically or through the less sophisticated process of dragging an anchor in the way the Kingston Branch were doing when they hooked the *Kyarra*. When trailing an anchor have one member of the team holding the line in order to feel when the anchor snags, so that power can be cut to prevent the line from parting. When drag searching an area it is essential to proceed slowly or the anchor may lift off the bottom and miss the wreckage completely.

An echo sounder which prints a trace on a moving paper band, the easiest and most satisfactory search method if the budget will run to it. These instruments may be hard to interpret when being operated over a rocky seabed which provides large numbers of difficult to classify traces.

Metal Detection

There are two types of detector, a magnetometer used from the search vessel and metal detectors which are used for undersea sweeps and are of more value when hunting the remains of older wrecks which are completely buried under sand or silt.

Magnetometers measure the earth's magnetic field and detect distortions caused by the presence of ferrous objects. The signal is displayed on the dial of a receiver or on a moving paper trace. A typical instrument which uses a "proton" detector head is said to be capable of detecting amounts as small as 1.5 tons of ferrous metal at a depth of fifty feet or 50 tons at 132 feet. Magnetometers are hard to use if only small amounts of ferrous metals are involved, and problems can arise when operating over uneven seabeds and outcrops of volcanic rocks which may cause similar distortions to a man made source. When using a magnetometer it is important to keep the speed of the search vessel low or small objects may be missed, and to bear in mind that because of the earth's magnetic field objects which can be detected on a North/South search may remain undetected on an East/West track.

There are a variety of metal detectors on the market suitable for underwater use. A metal detector works on the principle that a metal object moving through a magnetic field, created by passing an electric current through a coil of wire, causes variations in the current which can be recorded as a change in sound frequency, the movement of a needle on a dial or a light. The average seabed depth at which small objects such as coin can be detected is about a foot, although cannon should be detected at eight or ten feet using a suitably sensitive instrument.

Because sea water is a good conductor of electricity metal detectors based on a high frequency oscillator system suffer severe signal loss and are not suitable for underwater work. The best uses a high current pulse transmitter and is known as a Pulse Induction detector. A commercially available Pulse Induction detector is the Aquatec which is sensitive to both ferrous and non-ferrous metal, and can detect coins the size of a penny at a depth of 12 " and cannon down to 10 feet. During trials in the North Sea a well-head was detected at a depth of twenty feet. Such an instrument is probably more valuable to archaeologists whose approach to wreck detection I shall discuss in the next chapter, but it can play its role in locating scattered and encrusted pieces of debris from modern wrecks as well.

Survey

Once a wreck has been located the next step is to make a complete but cautious preliminary survey. If the wreck is a large one orientate yourself carefully before leaving the static reference point, probably the anchor rope. As in navigation across the seabed, note distinctive features of the wreckage so that you will be able to return easily to your starting point. During this first survey get an overall idea of the size, shape and condition of the vessel. Beware of jagged plates and sharp angles of steel as they can snag or damage your equipment and inflict a nasty wound. Some wrecks are known to local anglers as good fishing areas and it is possible that the site will be draped in lengths of nylon fishing line. This may catch around equipment and parts of the body, and cannot be broken by pulling. Any attempt to do so will only damage your hands. Cut the line or get your diving partner to cut you free. Watch out for fish hooks which may be attached to the end of such lines as they can inflict a painful injury. If trawlers have operated in the area they may have snagged and lost their trawls around the wreck and these are even more hazardous than floating line. So keep a careful watch out for yourself and your partner.

When entering wrecks exercise extreme caution. Bulkheads weakened by years of immersion may be so paper thin that your bubbles could be sufficient to collapse them. As it will be pitch dark inside the wreck always use a powerful torch both to orientate yourself and to show up jagged obstacles and obstructions.

Salvage Operations

Cutting and lifting large sections of a wreck is a major operation. Small items, like the ship's bell, can be air-lifted to the surface using such items as old oil drums drilled to take lifting ropes or wires. These are taken down and fitted to the object which has to be raised and then filled with air from a spare diving cylinder. The procedure is relatively straightforward. But remember that as the container rises the pressure gets less and the air expands speeding up the rate of ascent to a point where the lift may get out of control. To prevent this arrange that the amount of buoyancy applied is a little less than that required to raise the object alone, the difference is made up by stout hearted men on the surface pulling at ropes. As a guide, a three gallon drum displaces about 31 lbs of water. If the drum weighs seven pounds it will therefore provide a lift of 24 lbs. Drums and buckets make particularly good lifting devices as the excess air, caused by expansion, simply spills out around the edges maintaining constant buoyancy all the way up. If a sealed lifting system is used the bags must be provided with venting valves to allow the expanding air to escape. The most critical moment of any lift is when the buoyancy system reaches the surface. If drums are used and overturn because the speed of ascent has been too rapid, all buoyancy is immediately lost and the object will vanish again into the depths, perhaps for ever.

For salvaging large wrecks, a knowledge of the use of underwater cutting techniques and explosives may be required. These techniques are taught on courses run at Fort Bovisand in Plymouth. Based on an old Napoleonic fort which overlooks Plymouth Sound, Bovisand has its own private harbour, as well as showers and a club room with a magnificent view across the Sound. At Fort Bovisand divers can also brush up their photography, learn marine biology, archaeology or boat handling. The courses are arranged over weekends or for longer periods. Fort Bovisand which came into being through the determination of two divers, Alan Bax and Jim Gill, is now the foremost diving centre in England. For details of their courses you should write to Plymouth Ocean Projects, Fort Bovisand, Plymouth PL9 OAB (Telephone: Plymouth 42570).

Further Reading

The Wreck Hunters: Roger Jefferis and Kendall McDonald. George Harrup, London, 1966. Good description of wrecks and salvage operations.

Cornish Shipwrecks: Richard Larn and Clive Carter. David and Charles, 1969–71. Three volumes. A valuable reference for West Country wrecks. The volumes cover both North and South coasts and includes the Isle of Scilly.

Shipwrecks Around Britain: Leo Zanelli. Kaye and Ward. London, 1972. List of wrecks, more that 400 of them, around British shores.

Jutland to Junkyard: S. C. George. Patrick Stephens Ltd. London, 1973. Interesting account of the mammoth salvage task of recovering scrap metal from the German Imperial Fleet which was scuttled at Scapa Flow.

The Wreck Detectives: Kendall McDonald. George Harrap. London, 1972. Excellent descriptions of wreck hunting operations and a valuable reference section which deals with locating wrecks, and salvage law.

8

Underwater Archaeology

On September 21st, 1588 the *Santa Maria de la Rosa* was not a happy ship. In May when she had sailed proudly as part of the Spanish Armada, vice-flagship of the squadron of Guipuzcao, in a convoy commanded by the Duke of Medina Sidonia, the Spaniards had been confident of a swift victory. By mid-summer, English Naval power, unfavourable weather, and disease had combined to shatter any hope of success and all the Spanish crew now prayed for was the chance to limp home in peace.

The *Santa Maria de la Rosa*, laden with cannon "fifty great pieces all of the field" was also weighted down by silver and gold ducets and a fortune in plate, the property of wealthy officers who had expected an easy conquest.

Her hull, damaged by skirmishes with British warships, was taking in water and her sails were in tatters as the *Santa Maria* sailed sluggishly around the west coast of Ireland. Food was in short supply and what little there was had rotted, the drinking water was filmed with green scum and stinking, the crew decimated by injury and disease. The violent storm which struck on September 21st was the final disaster for the exhausted Spaniards, and the *Santa Maria*'s Captain decided to run for shelter in Blasket Sound. As she limped into the relatively calm waters between Great Blasket Island and the mainland, her lookout called excitedly that two other Spanish vessels had also sought sanctuary from the storm. The *Santa Maria* fired a cannon to attract their attention. It was mid-day.

Aboard one of the other ships, the San Juan of the Castille Squadron, her Commander Marcos de Aramburu observed the *Santa Maria* arrive and noted: "She had all her sails torn to ribbons except the foresail. She anchored with a single anchor, as she had no more. And as the tide, which was coming in from the south-east, beat against her, she held on 'till two o'clock when it began to ebb, and at the turn she commenced drifting, about two splices of cable from us, and we with her; and in an instant we saw she was going to the bottom while trying to hoist the foresail and immediately she went down with the whole crew, not a soul escaping—a most extraordinary and terrible occurrence."

The *Santa Maria de la Rosa* had struck an uncharted rock and took all but one of her crew, he was washed ashore on a plank naked and near death, to the bottom a hundred feet below.

I have described the last few hours of the *Santa Maria* in some detail because the discovery of this wreck and excavations that followed provide a perfect example of how such operations ought to be carried out.

The sea conditions in Blasket Sound make for dangerous and difficult diving. The tides are strong, there are fast currents and visibility is poor. In 1963 a diver drowned whilst exploring the area. In 1965 Syd Wignall, a mountaineer turned skin-diver, obtained an exclusive five year licence from the Madrid authorities to excavate the wreck. He had always been fascinated by the story of the *Santa Maria* and was determined to locate and scientifically explore the wreck. His first expedition to Blasket Sound in 1963 had been fruitless and it wasn't until a major search was mounted in 1968 that the wreck was finally located. The system used, which involved close co-operation between the volunteer members of a large diving team, enabled more that 3,000 acres of seabed to be thoroughly searched. The first discovery was the uncharted rock on which the *Santa Maria* had come to grief. It came so close to the surface that a diver standing on top could put his hands out of the water.

The next was an odd pile of stones resting on the bottom. They looked like part of the seabed scenery until a diver hammered at one with his knife and found that it was made of iron. The stones were heaps of cannonballs! The following year the expedition went back to Blasket Sound. This time, using a metal detector, they made the first really exciting find, a large pewter plate under which a human skeleton and the remains of a purse containing silver and gold coins were discovered. On the plate was stamped the name of the Captain of Infantry aboard the *Santa Maria*.

At a depth of 120 feet, large well preserved parts of the vessel were found, providing a time-capsule which gave historians information about the way the sailors and soldiers of Philip's Armada lived and worked.

An account of the 1969 expedition, by Colin Martin was published in the Council for Nautical Archaeology's [C.N.A.] newsletter and provides an excellent example of how such reports should be compiled: "It was discovered that most of the lower forward section remained intact, and the scarf jointed keelson was traced for more than forty feet. Six tenoned uprights are positioned along this length, against which are placed two broad shifting planks, on edge one atop the other, intended to stabilise the stone ballast. A complex structure, identified as the stepping box of the mainmast, was uncovered on the keelson axis. Several points of interest emerged. The keelson here is considerably thicker than elsewhere, a strengthening feature mentioned in contemporary shipbuilding treatises. In addition, two flush supporting sleepers lie on either side of it. Three heavy riders, with squared off ends, evidently once butted into recesses in the stepping block itself, but this component, together with the heel of the mast, has ripped out, massively splintering the keelson to which it was bolted.

"Two types of iron fastening were identified. Wrought iron bolts, up to two and a half feet long, had been used to bind the major structural component, and also to secure the butt ends of outer planking, were special strength was required. The bolts have annular rivet heads, tightened by driving a wedge into a split in each bolt rod end. The bolt heads were seated on leather washers . . .

"Amongst the concretion surrounding the arquebuses two pewter plates were found in fine condition. Both were shallow dishes 8 " in diameter, and both were inscribed, on the underside of the rim, with the work *Matute*. This name occurs in the fleet muster held at Lisbon on May 14th, 1588 as Francisco Ruiz Matute, an infantry captain in the Sicilian Tercio (regiment) under Don Diego Pimental . . .

"A considerable amount of brushwood and charcoal among the ballast just forward of the stepping box indicates a possible location for the galley fire. Absence of debris from the brickwork oven usually associated with shipboard galleys (e.g. Vasa) suggests that in this case the fire may have been open, laid directly on the ballast stones. So primitive an arrangement, if indeed it were such, lends meaning to the Duke of Medina Sidonia's strict instruction that galley fires were to be dowsed at sunset.

"This area also yielded quantities of bone and pottery. The bones were predominently those of sheep and cattle, with some chicken, and these no doubt came from the salted carcasses listed in the Armada inventories. That occasional luxuries, however, supplemented the monotonous and unhealthy diet is revealed by the find, in surprising condition, of a brazil nut."

Even in these brief extracts from the account of the painstaking work done on the *Santa Maria*, several points emerge. The first is how much detailed information, on subjects ranging from ship building to the social conditions aboard ship, can be discovered by the proper excavation of a major wreck site. The second is the care which must be taken in noting down every find, however small and apparently trivial and its relationship to other artefacts as well as the location within the total wreck site. Records in the form of reports, plans, drawings made on plastic pads on the site, and photographs in black and white and colour are all essential if the full value of the wreck is to be assessed.

One of the main problems facing inexperienced divers is actually identifying a site. On the *Santa Maria* it was the black clouds of iron escaping from a knife grazed "boulder" that revealed it as an iron cannonball. Concretion, together with weed and all types of marine growth can disguise a wreck so effectively that it may be missed by the most experienced and observant diver archaeologist. Sometimes the only visible signpost to a buried wreck may be a lone cannonball resting on the bottom. When such a discovery is made the temptation to snatch up the find and head for the surface is tremendous, but it must at all costs be resisted or the whole site may be lost for ever. It should never be assumed that the cannonball was merely dumped over the side to lighten ship in a storm, or fired in battle. The correct procedure is to mark the spot as carefully as possible, ideally by placing a small buoy above the find. If the discovery is made on a routine dive it is unlikely you will be carrying such a useful aid, so the next best thing is to surface and take careful bearings on land marks in the way described in the last chapter, either visually or with a compass. If you have a camera then shoot some photographs so that the exact spot can be located at a later date using the pictures as reference.

Once you have located a possible wreck site the next stage is search and research. At sea use one of the techniques described below to comb the area, on land go through old records to try and identify the vessel. Local newspapers, ancient charts and museums in the area may provide some clues, reference sources in London which are listed at the end of this chapter can supply others.

If your subsequent work suggests that you have indeed stumbled on a historic wreck then you should inform the Council for Nautical Archaeology. Your letter should give your name, address and phone number, the date of discovery and the approximate position of the find. You should include a description of the find, a sketch and measurements if possible, together with an account of diving conditions, seabed and plant life on the site.

If you discover cannon on the site these can be an extremely valuable method of dating the wreck, as will be any coins. The main parts of a cannon are shown on the accompanying illustrations. A cannon record form should look something like this:

SITE   DATE   NO   BRONZE/IRON

Width at:- BREECH   TRUNNION   MUZZLE

Overall Lengths: Bore

Mouldings from Breech   Total Number
0–1   1–2   2–3   3–4   4–5   5–6   6–7

Pommellion   Cascabelle

Sketch

Search Techniques
Bear in mind that artefacts and the remains of historic wrecks are likely to be heavily camouflaged by marine growth and sediment. Watch out for unnaturally straight lines or curves on the seabed. Do not overlook the slightest clue. When anything interesting is found examine it

84

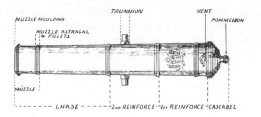

Fig. 5. A cannon showing the main sections and mouldings which must be recorded for an accurate identification.

carefully but do not remove it from the site. Mark the spot with a small buoy which you should always carry during serious search operations.

There are three basic search methods when large areas have to be covered. The system used to cover 3,200 acres of seabed during the hunt for the *Santa Maria* was the *Freeline Search Technique*. This enables large areas to be examined thoroughly and reasonably quickly, but it requires a high degree of co-ordination and discipline amongst the divers involved. A number of divers, up to fourteen have taken part in one search, are spaced out along a search line at a distance apart equal to twice the visibility. Four buoys mark the corners of the oblong search area. The men at either ends and the centre man, who controls the line, each carry buoy markers so that the progress of the moving line of divers can be watched from the surface.

In the *Towed Method* one diver carries out the search and is pulled along attached to a line from the diving boat or lying flat on an underwater sledge. It is essential that the diver's speed be kept as low as possible or he will miss clues even in reasonable visibility. Alan Bax who runs archaeological courses at Fort Bovisand, points out during his lectures that one knot over the ground is equal to 100 feet a minute or 1.6 feet a second. Given ten foot visibility this means the diver has only about six seconds to assimilate what he sees.

As with the *Freeline Method* the search area must first be marked out with buoys and the diver then towed over a series of parallel laps. Alternatively, if the visibility is low, a zig-zag tow can be used which allows for overlap of the area previously examined. When using the two-line method it must be borne in mind that divers are liable to chill far more rapidly than when involved in energetic work. Cold not only speeds up the onset of exhaustion but it rapidly lowers the ability to concentrate. Divers should not therefore remain underwater for extended periods when working in northern waters.

The third method is the *Fixed Line Search* which is useful in low visibility or where heavy marine growth obscures the seabed. Two parallel lines are laid down, they should be of a material like white nylon to make them easily visible, and joined by a light line which is weighted at each end. Two divers carry out the search, swimming towards one another on either side of the light line. When they each come to the end of the light line it is moved forward a short distance along the parallel lines and the next section of the search area examined.

Metal detection equipment, described in the previous chapter, can prove a very valuable aid to successful searchers as the Blasket Sound expedition discovered.

Records

On site sketches are often essential and should be made by means of a wax pencil and sheets of plastic. Such an underwater sketch pad should form part of your basic survey equipment. It can be made up quickly and cheaply.

Details about each dive must be carefully recorded including such information as the objectives achieved, the names of those involved, the weather and sea conditions. Every find must be noted as it is lifted and before lifting, it should be carefully photographed and sketched *in situ*. Plans must include an initial scale drawing of the site, and development drawings as the site is excavated.

The camera is an extremely valuable tool in underwater archaeology and the whole wreck site should be photographed before any work is begun. It will almost certainly be necessary to do this by mosaic photography, building up a view of the area with a large number of single pictures. When taking these shots be careful to maintain the same height above the site for each, and allow plenty of overlap. These pictures are best taken in black and white, which is satisfactory for most record work during the excavations although some colour pictures can be helpful and certainly makes the records look more interesting. Each picture must contain a properly calibrated scale. Putting a diving knife into the photograph to provide a crude size comparison is not good enough. A rod marked out in black and white intervals with an arrow painted at one end, so that it can be aligned along a compass bearing, is an essential piece of equipment.

Before attempting mosaic photography the area must be marked off into a grid pattern using tapes stretched taut between "bench marks". Rock climbers pitons can be driven into rocks to hold these tapes, or lead weights used on any fairly even sand or silt bottom. Swim steadily across the grid area taking pictures as you go.

Clearing Sites

No artefact must be removed until it has been photographed and recorded. Rubbish cluttering up the site, rocks, boulders, weeds and so on, should be removed and carried well clear of the search area to prevent them drifting back onto the site. However, disturbance of the seabed must be kept to an absolute minimum and nothing, plant or boulder that it is not essential to shift out of the way should be tampered with.

Large rocks may have to be broken up, perhaps with explosive, before they can be removed. If explosive is used it must be handled with caution to avoid damaging any artefacts. Small boulders can be lifted clear by hand, and such loose material as pebbles collected up in bags and removed. Sand and silt may be blown clear of a wreck site using water jets.

Conservation

Material which has survived for centuries under the sea deteriorates rapidly when brought into contact with air, so preparations for the treatment of large finds, such as cannon, must be made long before the objects are raised. If expert treatment for a particular item cannot be arranged then it is far better left on the bottom until such time as conservation can be properly carried out. Considerable damage was done to interesting finds removed from the 18th century wreck of H.M.S. *Association*, a ninety gun ship-of-the-line off the Scilly Isles because they were not treated after being removed from the site.

Where objects like cannonballs are concerned thick concretion should be removed by tapping with a hammer, thinner layers can be removed in a bath of 10% nitric acid. This acid bath can also be used to remove growths from pottery, once the salt has been washed away in fresh water.

Water, distilled rather than ordinary tap water which contains chlorine, can also be used to preserve glass and such organic material as leather, wood and bone. The objects should be soaked in regularly changes of fresh water until all the salt has been removed.

The cleaning of coins is a job which should be left to the experts. Your local museum will probably be able to advise on the preservation of finds, if not write for help to the Committee for Nautical Archaeology.

In an article in *The Guardian* newspaper in 1971, I remarked that the year had been a good one for piracy and a disastrous one for marine archaeology, with the looting of valuable wreck sites up and down the coast of Britain. At that time experts were predicting the loss of all wooden wreck sites within ten years, and since these number several hundreds of thousands, the picture seemed gloomy indeed. Since then the situation has improved a little, as the completely out dated Merchant Shipping Act has been amended to protect valuable wreck sites. At present, however, this legal protection has only been extended to eight sites; including the Amsterdam, a Dutch East Indiaman which lies on the shore near Hastings; the *Mary Rose*, Henry VIII's flagship which foundered off Spithead in 1545; the *Mary*, Charles II's yacht lost near Anglesey in 1575 and the *Grace Dieu*, an early 15th century British warship lying in the river Hamble. It may not be much, but at least the Protection of Wrecks Act is a start.

The best protection for our uniquely valuable wreck sites lies in diver education. All too often it is not greed but ignorance that leads to artefacts being lifted and sites lost.

If you want to become actively involved in archaeology, you should help to support this work of education and protection by becoming an associate member of the Nautical Archaeology Trust which was formed by the C.N.A. in 1972. The Council itself was formed in 1964 and its membership includes divers, archaeologists, representatives from the National Maritime Museum, British Museum, Science Museum, Institute of Archaeology, Society for Nautical Research, the British Sub Aqua Club, and others. The C.N.A.'s and the Trust's aims are to promote research into Nautical Archaeology at home and abroad, to encourage training in underwater archaeology, to safeguard underwater discoveries and to liaise between divers, historians and archaeologists. Their address is: C.N.A., Institute of Archaeology, 31–34 Gordon Square, London WC1. They also have regional representatives who may be contacted when a find is made in their area.

Eire   Miss Celia O/Rahylly, Cursis Stream Palmerstown, Co. Dublin, Eire.
Lincs and Notts   Mr Nigel Kerr, 28 Belton Lane, Grantham, Lincs.
North East   Mr Alan Binns, University of Hull.
North West   Dr P. N. Davies, University of Liverpool.
Scotland   R. B. K. Stevenson, National Museum of Antiquities, Edinburgh.
South East   Miss Joan Du Plat Taylor, 11 Fox Road, Balsham, Cambridge.
South West   Professor Charles Thomas, Institute of Cornish Studies, Trevenson House, Poole, Redruth, Cornwall.
South Wales   Mr R. A. Kennedy, County Museum, Haverford West.
Somerset/Severn Basin   Mr David Blackman, University of Bristol.
Scilly Islands   Miss Sania Butcher, Hugh House, St. Mary's.
Sussex/Hampshire   Mrs Rule, Mill House, Westbourne, Emsworth.
Thames Estuary area   Mr Peter Marsden, The Guildhall Museum, London EC3.

Advice on cannon finds may be obtained from:

Austen C. Carpenter, Department of the Environment, 1–3 Albert Road, Devonport, Plymouth, Devon PL2 1AA.

H. L. Blackmore, Assistant Master of the Armouries, New Armouries, H.M. Tower of London, London EC3. When writing for information you should always enclose a stamped addressed envelope. Whether or not these experts can help you identify your cannon depends on how much information you can supply them. Unless the cannon is well preserved and remarkably free from concretions, only likely now and then in the case of bronze guns, positive identification will have to await raising and cleaning as good descriptions accompanied by all the measurements listed in the cannon report form will be needed.

Research Sources
In addition to those listed in the previous chapter the following may be able to provide clues in the case of vessels over a hundred years old.

The Public Records Office: Chancery Lane, London WC2A 1LR. This office contains a vast amount of information but it takes a little time to find your way around it! A temporary readers permit, valid for a week, can be obtained from the issuing officer provided you can produce some other form of personal identification. For more prolonged research a Readers Permit valid for three years will be needed. To obtain this you have to fill in an application form and get it signed by somebody like a doctor or solicitor. If you are at University then the signature of a lecturer or college secretary will be satisfactory. The rooms are open from 9.30 a.m. to 5.00 p.m. Amongst the valuable documents held in the PRO are accounts of court-martials. As these often followed the sinking of a Navy vessel they can provide extremely important sources, giving exact dates, circumstances of the loss and locations. These records start in 1880.

Customs House Library: Kings Beam House, 38–41 Mark Lane, London EC3 7IIE. Here you can find ships registers going back to early 1700.

For Further Reading
Marine Archaeology. Joan Du Plat Taylor. Hutchinson and Co., London, 1965. A standard work on the subject by a world expert. Contains descriptions of excavations and artefacts, well illustrated with photographs and drawings.
Nautical Archaeology. Bill St. John Wilkes. David and Charles, 1971. A good practical guide with a section on preservation.
Underwater Archaeology. P. E. Cleator, Robert Hale, 1973. Interesting on the history of underwater archaeology and descriptions of site operations.
The Treasure Hunters Guide. John S. Potter. Robert Hale, 1972. Good descriptions of artefacts, including weapons, and list of notable wrecks around the world.
Cities in the Sea. Nicholas C. Flemming. New English Library, 1972. Fascinating account of the exploration of submerged cities around the world.
Mary Rose—Its Fate and Future. Alexander McKee. Souvenir Press, 1973. A story of one man's determination and the dedication of many divers who worked with Alexander McKee in the excavation of the site

of Henry VIII's flagship. This could be the most important find to date off our coasts and the book gives a daunting insight into the problems confronting serious underwater archaeologists.

Pieces of Eight. Kip Wagner. Longmans, 1968. An exciting story of the salvage of Spanish gold from the Florida reefs.

History Under the Sea. Alexander McKee. Hutchinson, 1968. First class reference book based on practical experience.

The Divers Swimline Search. British Sub Aqua Club Paper Number 2. By Commander J. Grattan the man who organised the search operation which found the *Santa Maria de la Rosa.*

As I mentioned at the end of the last chapter, Fort Bovisand run a course on underwater archaeology which provides lecture room and practical work.

9

Marine Biology

During your early dives the sea may appear a fairly deserted environment. Perhaps a shoal of pouting, the sparrows of the ocean, may drift into view, and a frantic scurrying across a patch of exposed sand occasionally betray the presence of a small crab. In dark recesses you may encounter the baleful gold-rimmed gleam of a conger or suddenly realise that the hideous gargoyle formation of rock before you is a living creature, the angler fish quietly awaiting its victim. In the last two cases inexperienced divers—and many not so inexperienced divers—may find their air consumption shoot up as they shoot off as fast as fins will take them.

But frequently first dives in northern waters prove slightly uninteresting. There is plenty of seaweed to be sure, great brown fronds waving in the current, but where is all the marine life you had expected? It is there alright, probably watching you with a hundred sets of eyes from a hundred covers and crevices in the rocks and weeds. The fact that it remains all but invisible is more a tribute to the brilliance of sub-aqua camouflage than a slight on your powers of observation.

Take the angler fish, for example, probably one of the ugliest creatures you will encounter in northern waters. Most divers only notice the fish, which can grow up to 100 lbs in weight and almost six feet in length, when they are right on top of the vast, semi-circular mouth with its row of irregularly spaced teeth. The angler's camouflage has to be good, not to take visiting divers by surprise, but because his lunch depends on other fish mistaking him for an inanimate object. His name derives from the fact that he uses a fleshy lobe at the end of the first dorsal ray as a fishing line. Small fish, flatfish, haddock and dogfish, who investigate this enticing morsel suddenly find themselves on the menu. You will find anglers half buried in mud or sand or lurking amongst seaweeds. Their loose skin helps break up their outlines and the blotches of brown, reddish brown and greenish brown blend them with their surroundings.

The angler's camouflage is extremely effective but the systems evolved by other fish may be even more subtle. Take for example the silver flanks of many open water fish. Seen on a flash photograph the gleaming scales would seem to provide anything but a camouflage. In fact they are an extremely effective form of concealment. Beneath the surface, light arriving from any horizontal direction is more or less equal. A mirror suspended in the water is virtually invisible when seen from straight on. The curved surface of the fish uses small, reflecting crystals so arranged in each scale that the whole curved body acts as a mirror. Seen from above, such a wide mirror would be all too obvious were it not for the fact that light sensitive cells in the scales covering the upper surface adjust to match the brightness and colour of the dim waters below. The only situation in which this brilliant and ever changing camouflage is helpless is when the fish is seen from below. Under most other conditions he remains extremely hard to detect.

Once you become more familiar with the underwater scene and diving techniques have become second nature, you find your powers of observation sharpen. Within a short space of time the world which seemed so devoid of life is transformed. How sharp an experienced diver's eyes become was illustrated for me during a dive off the island of Gozo in the Mediterranean with a great diving companion, Ian Boyd. We were finning along over a rocky seafloor at about thirty feet in perfect visibility, Ian's particular interest is underwater archaeology and on this dive he was looking out for fragments of amphora. Suddenly he plunged headfirst into a gloomy weed fringed rock crevice about six feet below the level of the seafloor. A second later he was gently lifting a small section of amphora from the surrounding growth. It was so heavily disguised by weed and crustaceans that I would have swum over the area a hundred times within inches of the artefact without spotting it. This particular piece of amphora turned out to be the home of an octopus who became extremely angry that his comfortable home was suddenly removed. For a moment the sea around Ian's mask was churned into a fury of black squirted ink and undulating limbs. Then the octopus decided to give him best and jetted off into the weeds. Had Ian been interested in octopus rather than amphora he would himself have found himself a first class specimen.

So the first essential for a diver who wants to specialise in marine biology is plenty of year round underwater experience. Seasonal changes occur below the waves as above, and plants which you identify easily in springtime may look completely different in winter. Fish too change their habitats, some deep sea varieties may spend part of the year in shallower coastal waters, when the summer sunlight is strong creatures who can normally be found quite easily hide under rocks and weed.

The area in which the diver/biologist has probably the greatest contribution to make is in the serious observation of species on their own territory. The skin diver has the chance, never available before the development of SCUBA equipment, to study feeding habits, courtship, response to predators, camouflage methods and the relationship of one species to another, under natural conditions. All that is required is patience and some fairly easily acquired skills.

Inevitably, a time will come when species have to be taken either as live specimens to be kept under closer observation in an aquarium or for

92

killing and preservation. It is essential that removal of any form of marine life be kept to a minimum. It would only need each diver who visits a particular area to remove a few anemones (or more probably a lobster!) for the location to be decimated of that species. Collecting should be undertaken thoughtfully and with a specific purpose in mind. Large fish can be netted, small specimens sucked up into a "slurp gun." This is a large bore tube fitted with and plunger and piston. When the piston is pulled back the fish is drawn into the cylinder. Robust specimens can be kept in bags, while delicate creatures should be placed in plastic containers. When collecting weeds, and rock clinging animals a knife can be used quite satisfactorily although it is advisable to wear gloves when handling some species, for example sea urchins.

Preserving
Decay sets in rapidly after death so preserving solutions should be on hand in the diving boat or immediately after landing. Fish, octopus, jellyfish and sea-anemones can be preserved in a 5 or 10% solution of formalin. Crustaceans can be killed in a 70% solution of alcohol. The soft internal organs should be removed and the species can then be preserved in 10% formalin for up to three days, depending on the size of the specimen. After that they should be removed and pinned to cork or board. A coat of colourless varnish will help preserve the shells.

Starfish can be killed in 30% alcohol, then transferred to a 10% formalin solution for up to four days, again it depends on the size of the specimen, before being allowed to dry into shape. The authors W. De Haas and F. Knorr advise a slightly different solution for preserving these creatures after killing. They claim that it gives better results from the point of view of colour and shape with the spiny starfish and the common starfish: 50 g. alum. 12 g. common salt, 10 g. saltpetre, 30 g. potash and 5 g. arsenic in 1.5 litres of boiling water. After cooling the solution should be filtered and 600 cc of glycerine and 1,700 cc of methyl alcohol added. The specimens are left in this solution for between 5 and 8 days. *This solution must be handled with care as it is poisonous.*

Fish can be killed with acetic chloroform and then washed in soda solution to remove the slime. They should be fixed for between two and three days in a 10% formalin solution and then preserved in 1% solution of phenoxtetol.

Seaweeds
These can be dried after rinsing in sea water. Place them in water in a flat dish lined with a sheet of thick, non-glazed, paper. When the weed has assumed the shape required lift the paper gently clear of the dish. Press between sheets of newspaper to dry but make sure that not too much weight is used or it may transfer the specimen to the mounting paper.

To be of any value specimens should be clearly identified and a record of the sea area, depth of water, sea conditions and any other relevant information carefully preserved.

Sea Aquarium
Species can be kept alive for study, although maintaining a satisfactory marine aquarium is a far more difficult task than keeping a fresh water one. Some species, small fish, crabs, anemones and lobster can survive in still salt water which is aerated by an efficient pump. Many salt water species however require a constant supply of sea water which is fresh, cool and well aerated and maintaining these condition in a tank can be complicated and expensive. However, the following hints may help to avoid early fatalities.

Tanks: As corrosion proof as possible, salt resistent steel or Monel Metal should be used for the frame. Have as large a tank as possible and do not overstock.

Water: If you live by the sea it may be possible to fill the tank with the real thing. Preferably the water should be collected from a boat to avoid the risk of contamination. If this is not feasible the water should be allowed to stand for several hours and then siphoned off to remove any suspended material. Water must be collected in a non-toxic, non-corrosive container such as a plastic bucket. It can be transported in polythene bags.

There are now a number of brands of artificial salt water mixes available. Th manufacturers instructions should be carefully followed and the mixture allowed to stand before use.

Whichever type of water you use always make certain that you have a reserve supply of clean water for use in case the tank becomes polluted. If this happens it may only be the swift transfer of species of fresh, pure water that will save your collection.

Temperature: Must be accurately maintained for tropical fish, it is less critical for northern water species who are used to a wider temperature variation.

Specific Gravity: Measured with a hydrometer. Most fish can tolerate a wide range of specific gravity. Coral fish are accustomed to 1.025, or a 3.5% salt content.

Pollution: Can be chemical or biological, in either case you will have to act quickly to save your specimens. The first indication of pollution are usually erratic and often frantic behaviour on the part of the fish. Chemical pollution can come from paint, detergent or cleaning solutions used in the tank or toxic metals in contact with the water. The source must be located or changing the water will only delay disaster.

Biological pollution can be recognised by the milky appearance which the water assumes. It is nearly always due to over-feeding or by the death of one of the specimens. The bloom and the odour are caused by bacteria which use up the oxygen in the water. Filters are not usually capable of dealing with the by-products of such pollution and the only answer is to change the water.

Filters: A good capacity filter is essential. One expert, William P. Braker of the Shedd Aquarium, Chicago, says that: "It is not possible to over-filter your tank but marine aquaria are frequently underfiltered. The minimum filtering rate should be a complete turnover once every four hours, but this will give you no margin for an emergency. If you can provide a filter or filters that will turn over the tank every two hours, so much the better, and once an hour is ideal." Such fast filtration provides the current flow which many marine species require. When it comes to buying the filtration and aeration equipment for a marine aquarium, expert advice from a qualified dealer should always be sought.

Aeration: This not only adds oxygen to the water but keeps the water moving, bringing the oxygen short water to the surface and the oxygen heavy water to the bottom. Strong aeration also helps to reduce the level of carbon dioxide in the water. Some collectors fail to realise that even though the oxygen content of their tanks may be sufficient species will still die if the carbon dioxide level is such that it interferes with their up-take of oxygen.

pH: This is a measure of the acidity or alkalinity of the water. The pH scale runs from 0–14, seven being neutral and anything above seven alkaline. Anything below seven is considered acid. The normal pH of saltwater is 8.3 and aquarium water should not be allowed to fall below 8.0. Checks can easily be carried out using an inexpensive kit. A drop towards the acid levels may indicate an excess of carbon dioxide in the water or the non-functioning of a filter layer.

Feeding: Preferably fish should be fed a little at a time throughout the day as this corresponds most closely with their normal habits. As this is usually impractical the next best thing is to establish a feeding routine, providing food at fixed periods three times a day for example, and then stick to it. Do not overfeed as it pollutes the tank.

These guidelines give an idea of the complexity of keeping an efficient marine aquarium. On the other hand the rewards can be great and enable effective observations to be carried out over a long period. But it must be emphasised that the taking of species, even if they are to be kept alive, is to be avoided unless there are good reasons for doing so.

Classification
Prior to the 18th century, creatures, if they were considered interesting enough to deserve any form of identification, usually got only a local

nickname. As methods of transport improved the fact that a fish or bird had one name in one place and a totally different name a few miles along the coast created obvious difficulties. A logical system was devised by a Swedish botanist, Carl von Linnaeus, and published in 1758. As Latin was the international language at that time the classification uses Latin names. By this system every creature has two names, a general one linking it to a group of closely related organisms, and one specific to that species. The system of classification exists to this day, in order to find your way casily around reference books, an understanding of it is valuable. The animal kingdom is divided into five grades of organisation and these grades are sub-divided into the major groups. *Phyla*. Each *Phylum* is divided into a number of Classes. Classes may be divided into *Sub-Classes* and further divided beyond this into *Orders* and then into *Families* and finally into *Genera*. The species is first given its generic name, which has a capital letter, and then the specific name with a small letter. For example the herring is *Clupea harengus*, while the sprat is *Clupea sprattus*.

The numbers of species embraced by the largest of all classifications, the Phylum, may be very large and diverse. For example fish belong to the *Phylum Chordata*, meaning animals which, at some time in their evolution, had a nerve cord running along the dorsal side of the body. In this Phylum in addition to fish comes man, birds and reptiles, but not for example, insects. The *Phylum Chordata* has four Sub-Phylums and it is to the last of these, the Sub-Phylum *Vertebrata*, that fish belong. This Sub-Phylum is further divided into two Superclasses, verterbrates with no proper jaws and those with jaws, which obviously includes fish. This Superclass (*Gnathostomata*) is further divided into six classes. These include mammals, reptiles, amphibians, and two classes for fish, those with a cartilagenous skeleton, such as skates and sharks and those with a bony skeleton such as turbot and plaice.

When you look a fish up in a reference book, therefore, you may find all or just some of these various classifications. They may appear confusing at first, but one soon finds it easier to use the correct scientific name as this provides more information than the common name. Take for example Bream, a species commonly found when diving in the Mediterranean. A Bream is a Bream is a Bream and that name tells us little more about the species. If, however, we start to identify the different types of Bream we observe by their correct Latin names some interesting facts start to emerge. A Bream with two black, saddle-like blotches, one just before the tail (caudal fin) the other behind the eye and extending down the body to the pectoral fin, is commonly known as Two-Banded Bream, its Latin Name is Diplodus vulgaris. This tells us that it belongs to the genus *Diplodus*. So does White Bream—*Diplodus sargus*—which has seven or eight vertical bands and a dark spot on the tail stalk. However, another fish commonly called *Sheepshead Bream*, which tends to be a more solitary creature not forming shoals like the

A diver drops backwards into the Channel from his diving boat. (See chapter four)

A diver goes in feet first to explore the Mediterranean. (See chapter four)

Diver archaeologists at work fifty feet down in the Mediterranean, off Cyprus. (See chapter four)

A diver surfaces with his companion during some marine biology work in the Channel. Note the Nikonos camera carried to make on the spot records of weed growth. (See chapter five)

others, has the Latin name *Charax puntazzo*. In other words it belongs to a different genus (although a member of the same Family as the others) which means it must have anatomical differences as well as different social behaviour patterns. In fact the differences lie mainly in the way its teeth are formed. The proper classification and identification of species is fundamental to any scientific study of marine life. Another example may help to make the system clear. The White Shark, which I trust you will never have to identify at close quarters, has the specific name *rondeletii* and the generic name of *Carcharodon*. It would thus be written in a text book as *Carcharodon rondeletii*. It belongs to the family *Isuridae* of the order *Pleurotremata* and to the Class of *Chondrichthyes* or cartilagenous fishes which, as we saw belongs to the Sub-Phylum *Vertebrata* of the *Phylum Chordata*.

There are five Grades of Organisation divided into Phylums.

1. *PHYLUM PROTOZOA*: Single cell animals. e.g. Amoeba.
2. *PHYLUM COELENTERATA*: Multicellular radially symmetrical animals whose bodies are derived from two germ layers (diploblastic) e.g. Jelly fish, sea-anemones, coral polyps.
3. *PHYLUM PLATYHELMINTHES*: Multicellular bilaterally symmetrical animals with three germ layers (triploblastic) e.g. flat worms.
4. *PHYLUM ANNULATA*: Multicellular, bilaterally symmetrical, triploblastic animals with complex cell structures e.g. marine worms.

PHYLUM ARTHROPODA: Have hard external "skins" and jointed limbs. e.g. Crabs, lobsters. Also includes mosquitos, scorpions and spiders.

PHYLUM MOLLUSCA: e.g. Shell-fish, squid, octopus and cuttlefish.

PHYLUM ECHINODERMATA: e.g. Star-fish, sea urchins, sea-cucumbers

5. Multicellular, bilaterally symmetrical, triploblastic animals which have complex cell structures and have, or have had during their evolution a dorsally situated central nervous system.

PHYLUM CHORDATA: e.g. Fish, amphibians, reptiles, birds, mammals.

Phylum Chordata
Sub-Phylum
1. *Hemichordata*.
2. *Cephalochordata*.
3. *Urochordata*.
4. *Vertebrata*.

Vertebrata: This sub-phylum includes all creatures which have some degree of backbone and a nerve cord which elaborates into a brain contained in a head. The *Sub-Phylum Vertebrata* is further divided into two Super-Classes.

97

Superclass One
Vertebrates with no proper jaws, i.e. Lampreys

Superclass Two
Vertebrates with jaws. These are divided into six classes.

Class 1. (Elasmobranchii) Fishes with cartilagenous skeletons (sharks, skate rays).
Class 2. (Osteichthyes) Fishes with bony skeletons (plaice, cod, herrings).
Class 3. Amphibians.
Class 4. Reptiles.
Class 5. Birds.
Class 6. Mammals.

Further examples of the classification system in operation:

Class: Osteichtyes.
Order: Zeiformes—laterally flattened bodies, tall dorsal fins, large eyes.

Family: Mugilidae.
Genus: Mugil.
Specific Name: cephalus.
Written: Mugil cephalus.
Common name: Common Grey Mullet.

Specific name: auratus.
Written: Mugil auratus.
Common name: Golden Grey Mullet.

Order: Zeiformes.
Family: Zeidae.
Genus: Zeus.
Specific name: faber.
Written: Zeus faber.
Common name: John Dory.

Order: Isospondyli: Forked symmetrical tail, one dorsal fin.'
Family: Clupeidae.
Genus: Clupea.
Specific name: harengus.
Written: Clupea harengus.
Common name: Herring.

Genus: Clupea.
Specific name: sprattus.
Written: Clupea sprattus.
Common name: Sprat.

Order: *Heterosomata.* Includes all common flatfish. Fish lie
on their side with both eyes uppermost.
    Family: *Pleuronectidae.*
    Genus: *Pleuronectes.*
    Specific name: *platessa.*
    Written: *Pleuronectes platessa.*
    Common name: Plaice.

Genus: *Limanda.*
Specific name: *limanda.*
Written: *Limanda limanda.*
Common name: Dab.

Fish-watching

With a certain amount of practice it is possible to get very close to most
species of fish found in northern waters, which is just as well considering the low visibility. Kendall McDonald recounts how he once
tickled a John Dory after taking his photograph, and other divers have
reported baby congers rolling over like kittens to have their "stomachs"
scratched. Provided you do not have a spear-gun, fish seem to have a
sixth sense that enables them to differentiate between camera and gun,
friend and foe, you will be able to work your way up to most of them. An
exception is the haddock, an extremely nervous and rarely
photographed fish. One theory is that this species is sensitive to the high
pitched noise made by a diver's demand valve.

There are two chief methods of approaching fish. You can fish about
looking for them or you can allow yourself to drift with the tide. As fish
are often at their most interesting and obvious when they come out to
feed, during tidal flow, this second method has something to recommend it, as a great deal of sea floor can be explored with a minimum of
effort. However, stopping in one place to photograph or examine species
may be a problem unless you can apply the brake by grabbing an outcrop of rock. When drift-diving you should be attached to a large, easily
visible buoy so that those in the diving boat can easily follow your
progress. It is not enough to rely on them being able to see the exhaled
bubbles from your valve because the slightest chop on the surface makes
them almost impossible to match these accurately to the diver's
position.

When drift-diving, or finning, make sure that you are not negatively
buoyant or you will stir up silt and sediment making photography impossible and fish watching difficult. Swimming should be done smoothly

and the fins should not be allowed to drag along, or stir up, the sediment layers.

In addition to photography the marine biologist will need to take notes, if not *in situ* as soon as the diving boat is regained. Plastic slates, described in the previous chapter can be a help, although they will be hard to handle in addition to a camera. The type of fish and other marine life which you are likely to find will depend on the sea-bed conditions. Here is a brief guide to some of the species which make their home in different northern water conditions.

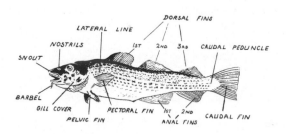

Fig. 6. A northern waters specimen showing the main parts of the external anatomy.

Rocks

Brown algae, seaweed, may be found in large quantities, on rocks, wreckage and submerged timbers. They are found down to depths of 120 feet. The brown colour is due to the presence of a pigment called fucoxanthin. A common variety is Sugar Kelp (*Laminaria saccharina*) which grows in leathery strands up to twelve feet long. This weed is found in the Channel, Atlantic, and North Sea. A weed with similar distribution is Bladder-Wrack (*Fucus vesiculosus*) which has ribbon like branches, with smooth edges and oval bladders. It is used in medicine and as a fertiliser. A fine, olive-brown string like weed, known as Mermaid's Fishline or Bootlace Weed (*Chordaria filum*) is often found twisted together like strands of rope and can measure twelve feet. A menacing sounding weed is Devil's Apron or Oar Weed (*Laminaria digitata*) which has a smooth stalk widening into a flat lobe which is slit into pliable bands. More delicate is Sphacelaria scoparia, a dark green feathery weed with brush shaped fronds. A lighter green weed is Sea Lettuce (*Ulva lactuca*) which has green leave like lobes which have irregularly shaped edges. This weed can be used as decoration in a marine aquarium, as can Cladophora sericea, which is dark green with delicate fronds.

Amongst these weeds and the rocks on which they grow can be found a variety of marine life, sponges, sea-anemones, marine worms, sedentary crustaceans, shrimps, crabs and lobsters. These last belong to the

Class Malacostraca in which there are 14,000 species.

Then there are the fish. Those you are most likely to see in Northern waters are:

Bib: Pout Whiting (Gadus luscus). I have described this fish briefly elsewhere, it is a very common companion to divers and may appear in large shoals. A dark fish with light bands which disappear as the fish grows older. The upper jaw is longer than the lower and it has a prominent barbel. They grow up to two feet long. Some have been observed with a white fungus in their mouths and it is feared but not confirmed that this may be the result of pollution.

Cod or Codling (Large fish or small fish (Gadus morhua). A large, dark fish which gives an impression of power and it can move very fast, so it needs to be stalked with care. The upper jaw is longer than the lower, the barbel is long. It has three dorsal fins and two anal fins, the tail fin is square. Young fish may be found in shallow water but the older fish have been located at depths down to 1,800 feet. There is a well defined courtship ritual which may be accompanied by grunting noises. In their natural state they live for up to ten years on average, although one cod was caught having survived to the ripe age of 24 years.

Conger (Conger conger). Can provide the uninitiated with a frightening encounter as I have already mentioned. They are said to be shy and not aggressive unless provoked. They live especially in wreckage or any habitat which will provide a dark retreat. They are found not only in the North Sea, Channel and Baltic but as far south as the Mediterranean. The body is powerful and elongated, the jaws large, the upper being a little longer than the lower. They have been found as deep as 3,000 feet although they also live happily in shallow water. They feed chiefly at night, mostly on bottom living fish, crustacea and cephalopods (cuttlefish, squid and octopus). The Northern European spans in midwinter at great depths.

John Dory (Zeus faber). Swims slowly with fins churning like a clockwork toy. There are two dark, distinctive marks on his side which legend claims is the thumb print left by St. Peter when he held the fish to remove the tribute money. Some reference books claim that this species is rare in British waters, a finding with which many skin-divers would disagree. This is an exotic looking fish and well worth photographing. A friendly creature he has a round, flattened body with the single dorsal fin trailing off into long filaments.

Sand and Mud
Plaice (Pleuronectes platessa). The plaice lives in sand where the colouring of a largely brown back spotted with yellow and brown,

101

provides a camouflage of sorts which the plaice often tries to improve by burying itself under a fine layer of sediment. Plaice spend the first twelve months of their lives in shallow water but when they have grown to a length of about six inches they move into deeper water. They feed on small crustaceans when young, shellfish such as cockles and small scallops when older. The teeth are especially well adapted for grinding up mollusc shells.

Dover Sole (*Solea solea*). The eyes in this species are on the right side of the head and the mouth is small and semi-circular. There is one long dorsal fin which starts at a point between the upper eye and the tip of the snout. The eye-side of the sole is brown with irregular blotches. They are found in shallow water and down to depths of 600 feet. During the winter they migrate to deep, off-shore water. They eat mainly at night with feeding peaks at dawn and dusk.

Angler Fish (*Lophius piscatorius*). Already described at the start of this chapter, another fairly common fish which will give the diver a shock on first encounter. The colouring is brownish or green-brown and mottled. One account claims they have been seen to attack seabirds on the surface and another observer says they creep along the seabottom using their pectoral fins, thus moving without disturbing the water while they hunt down their food which includes any bottom living animal. Spawning takes place in very deep water, possibly as deep as 400 feet.

Mediterranean fish (Rock and Weeds)
Grouper (*Epinephelus guaza*). Large fish with oval bodies and a lower jaw which protrudes slightly in front of the upper jaw. They have green brown backs with lighter sides and there is a light green mottling over the head, back and sides. The pectoral fins have dark edges, the dorsal fin has an orange edge. They have fixed habits and can spend years living in the same hole in the rock. Although they can grow up to four feet long, groupers can be found in shallow waters providing spearfishermen have not been in the area. They are curious by nature and will often swim over to investigate a diver. The species has been seriously depleted by "sportsmen" taking advantge of this boldness.

Sheephead Bream (*Charax puntazzo*). All species of Sea Bream are commonly found in the Mediterranean, especially near the coasts. Any oval bodied, silvery fish seen in this area is probably some species of bream. They have flattened bodies and small mouths set low in the head. The silvery body of the Sheepshead Bream has a number (up to eleven) of dark vertical stripes and a black spot on the tail. Most bream form shoals but the Sheepshead Bream is more likely to be encountered on its own. The eggs, which float, are laid in September and October. It can be found as deep as 150 feet.

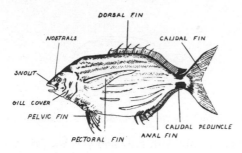

Fig. 7. A Mediterranean fish showing main parts of the external anatomy.

Scorpion Fish (*Scorpaena scrofa*). The most dangerous creature you are likely to encounter in the Mediterranean. It can cause a nasty wound by means of poison glands which lie at the base of the spiny rays. The treatment is to plunge the injured part into very hot water to ease the pain. Such wounds must be carefully cleaned and sterilised as they can go septic. The head of this fish is heavily armoured with spines, the body is sturdy and, above each oval eye there is a plume like appendage. They are reddish brown on the surface but beneath the sea this colour is not noticeable and they blend extremely well with their surroundings. They lie motionless on rocks in shallow water and it is easy enough to put your hand on one without realising it. They are carnivorous and feed at night. Eggs are embedded in a transparent mucous lump.

Note: When exploring rock surfaces watch out where you put your hand! If you are stung, even though the pain may not be immediate, get back to the surface as soon as possible. The onset of the pain can be delayed up to ten minutes but when it hits you will feel sick, faint and giddy.

Tropical Waters
Blue Shark (*Carcharchinus glancus*). This shark, which can occasionally be encountered in the Mediterranean, has a long (up to twelve feet) body and a long, pointed snout. There are distinctive pits immediately in front of the eyes. This species is nocturnal and lives mainly on fish, although it can be a man-eater. Over deep water they can be found near the surface. The young are born alive during the summer. Together with hammerheads they are the most commonly encountered shark.

Butterfly Fish. Several species belong to this family (*Chaetodon*) including the Grey Butterfly Fish, the Yellow Butterfly Fish and the Long-nosed Butterfly Fish. They are found on coral reefs and are all

103

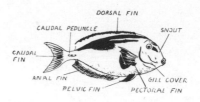

Fig. 8. A Tropical fish showing the main parts of the external anatomy.

brilliantly coloured, mainly with reds and yellows. Some have a thick stripe passing through the eye and a fake "eye" marking near the tail to confuse predators about the direction in which they will swim off. They grow to about nine inches in length. As a rule all these species are less shy in the presence of divers than another brightly coloured family of tropical fish, the Angel fish. Perhaps the most attractive of all Angel fish is the Emperor fish (*Pomacanthus imperator*) which grows up to a foot in length. They have a large number of orange yellow slightly diagonal lines running from head to tail. On the flanks the colours change to a glowing blue against a crimson background. They retreat rapidly in the presence of a diver.

From beauty to very much the beast of tropical waters a horror about which there is almost nothing good to say. This is the Stone Fish (*Synanceia verrucosa*) There are a number of species which can be found in tropical waters. They are ugly, clumsy and evil to look at, with gargoyle heads and squat bodies. They can often be encountered in shallow water and may easily be trodden on when paddling out over a reef. The head has a large mouth and small eyes hidden by flaps of skins and warts. This fish is extremely poisonous and can be fatal. The pain from their venom, delivered from glands beneath thirteen razor sharp dorsal spines, is excruciating. It only requires the slightest pressure to inject the venom. When pressed with a stick this poison has been observed to shoot four or five feet. Even stone fish which appear dead should be treated with the greatest caution. If attacked, immediate skilled medical attention is essential. The late Professor J. L. Smith who discovered the living fossil Coelacanth fish was attacked while at work in Kenya. He described the agony which followed as the worst he ever suffered. He treated himself with novocain and morphia by injection, but the greatest relief came from plunging his hand into very hot water. The water treatment was continued for some time until the pain had eased. Penicillin injections were later used to fight the infection but it was not until more than fifty days after the attack that the wound healed. I have discussed the Stone Fish in some detail in view of the information on tropical diving given in Chapter Ten. Prevention is better than cure where all dangerous creatures are concerned. Watch out were you put your hands and feet. Wear stout shoes when wading in reefs and use gloves for exploring coral and rock surfaces.

This brief guide to a few of the fishes should serve only as a scientific hors d'oeuvre, for the delights which await the diver/biologists on the sea-bed. Even if you only intend to take up marine biology to the extent of watching, identifying and photographing species, you will considerably increase your diving pleasure. However deep or superficial your interest the following books will provide fascinating reading:

Fish Watching and Photography (John Murray, London, 1972). Kendall McDonald and six other diver photographers have come together to produce a first class reference work packed with good photographs and based on practical experience of fish in their own world. It has very good chapters on the techniques of fish-watching and, as I mentioned at the end of Chapter Six, an excellent section on photography.

Fishes of the Sea (John and Gillian Lythgoe). Blandford Press, London, 1971. A rather more scholarly, but none the less readable guide to the fish found off the British Isles, Northern Europe and the Mediterranean. There are a large number of colour photographs, black and white shots and line drawings.

Under The Indian Ocean. Al. J. Venter. Nautical Publishing Company, Lymington, Hampshire, 1973. Interesting guide to diving around the Indian Ocean with descriptions of wrecks, marine life, encounters with sharks and stone fish, plus a fascinating guide to marine parks.

About Sharks and Shark Attack. David H. Davies. Routledge and Kegan Paul, London, 1965. Excellent guide to sharks and the research undertaken into these creatures. Some fairly horrific pictures of the consequence of shark attack. Not advisable to read this before a tropical dive!

Marine Life. W. De Haas and F. Knorr. A young specialist book published by Burke, London, 1966. A good guide to a wide variety of marine life, including sea-weeds, sponges and so on. A section on collecting and preserving material. Illustrated with black and white line drawings.

Collins Pocket Guide to the Sea Shore. John Barrett and C. M. Yonge. Collins, London, 1972. Contains clear descriptive material backed by more than 750 illustrations. A useful book for a diver with a family to entertain while he dives. The children can make their own discoveries in the rock pools.

How to Keep Salt Water Fishes. A useful and cheap guide which has some points of interest to those wanting to start up a marine aquarium although the emphasis is on tropical fish. William P. Braker, The Pet

Library Ltd., Fort Bovisand, Plymouth, which I mentioned earlier runs courses in marine biology and have their own laboratories at the Fort.

NOTE: Although the classification system was developed to standardise the naming of species it does not always work out like that. Sometimes a later authority will decide that a fish has been incorrectly named and change it. I have tried to give the most commonly used Latin names but you may find the same species differently described in some books.

10

Diving Around the World

There are three main ways of arranging a diving holiday. Which you select will depend on the type of diving that interests you, the country you want to visit and the amount of time you are prepared to spend in organising your trip.

The easiest way of arranging a diving holiday for the enthusiast who wants to spend more time underwater than sightseeing, is to book through one of the travel firms specialising in sub-aqua charters. Buying aircraft seats and hotel rooms in bulk they are able to provide the cost cutting facilities of normal charter firms with a guaranteed number of dives. Once you have paid your money, guides, air, equipment and boats will be assured.

This type of holiday is becoming increasingly popular but it fails to meet the requirements of two very different kinds of divers. The first is the holidaymaker who, perhaps because of family commitments, wants to spend more time in sunbathing and touring than diving. The second is the adventurous diver who wants to explore regions which are more or less unknown and undived.

Divers only interested in taking occasional trips beneath the surface will get better value by making local arrangements with commercial diving organisations or clubs, in the country they visit. They should take basic diving equipment, including demand valve but excluding cylinders and weight-belts, with them. Such on the spot arrangements are easy enough to make in areas like France, Malta, Spain, Italy and Cyprus where skin-diving is a popular tourist attraction. One drawback may be that your party may be made up of both experienced and novice divers which will limit the scope of expeditions.

The diver who likes to work new territory and dive from areas where there is only limited sports diving will be thrown back much more on his own organisational ability. With limited local sources of equipment to fall back on, such expeditions must take all the diving gear they need including a portable compressor, with them. This probably means transport by road since air freighting will prove extremely costly. These trips require a great deal of planning. Any diving organisations in the country chosen should be contacted to discover what permits will be needed and what prohibitions are in force. For the most part these will be connected with wreck sites of historic interest or the taking of fish from certain areas. Equipment must be chosen and packed with great care, something as trivial as a missing "O" ring can sabotage a dive completely in remote areas. Spare demand valves, weights, "O" rings, snorkels and masks should be packed and there should be a good supply of bottles so that a full day's diving can be enjoyed without wasting valuable daylight in recharging cylinders. Check the compressor, including the state of the filters, carefully before leaving and, if it has been working hard all year, get it serviced. Make certain you have a set of spare bolts, washers and couplings together with the necessary spanners and screwdrivers for carrying out running repairs.

If you intend to operate from really isolated bays and beaches then an inflatable will be a worthwhile addition to your equipment. This too must be carefully tested before being packed away.

The possibility of minor accidents must also be considered and a well stocked first aid kit taken. It is extremely useful if one of your party has some first aid experience. In most Middle East countries French is spoken as a second language and you will find French useful too in Greece and Turkey. It is worthwhile preparing a list of the main items of diving equipment in French before setting out.

If you fly with your equipment remember that cylinders must be emptied before aircraft companies will agree to fly them, and this applies to small bottles of ABLJs as well.

The information which follows includes details of diving clubs and hire services available in fifteen countries. From this list the reader will be able to judge those areas which provide facilities for on the spot diving with little or no pre-planning and those where considerable organisation will be required for satisfactory diving. Because advance booking reductions and charter flying have now brought virtually the whole world within reach of an increasing number of divers (for example a fortnight in Kenya at just over £200), I have not limited the list to those countries within easy reach of these shores. Great care has gone into preparing this information which is correct at the time of writing, but because organisations move and telephone numbers change, it is always best to check in advance if you intend to rely on them for your diving. Finally it must be pointed out that diving clubs abroad are under no obligation to help visiting divers. They usually do because there is a considerable comraderie between divers, but how much help is forthcoming will obviously depend on your personality and approach.

Diving Qualifications

If you hold a British Sub Aqua Club third class diving certificate, or above, then you should have no problems in diving around the world as these qualifications are respected by divers almost everywhere. In the absence of such qualifications you may be asked to prove your diving ability in a local pool or shallow water before divers or organisations are prepared to take you out. Such a test is only reasonable since any fool can claim diving ability, by the time his ignorance is discovered it may be too late, and some organisations are only insured when taking out qualified divers.

Membership of the BSAC also means that you have access to a wealth of diving experience around the world. If you are a member it is worth checking with the Club before any overseas trip, as they will be able to provide up to date information and put you in touch with divers who have been to that area before.

Algeria

With a 750 mile long Mediterranean coast line Algeria can offer a wide variety of interesting dives. It remains unspoilt and relatively un-explored underwater although the tourist industry is increasing fast and modern hotels are being built all along the coast. There are three sub-aqua organisations, listed below, who can help visiting divers with ad-vice and provide air. However, the best way to reach and explore the isolated diving areas is by car and boat. Camping is easy and cheap, as is simple accommodation in the small towns and villages. A vehicle and a portable compressor, plus a good supply of items like "O" rings are in-dispensible to any expedition. The main language is Arabic, but French is widely spoken and English understood by most officials in the main cities.

Underwater Organisations:
Widad Amal Casoral
Sports Sous-Marins Section
19 Bd Zirout Youcef
Algiers.

in Oran:

S.S.S.
B.P. 97 Oran *R.P.*

or:

Boutique du Club S.S.S.
6 rue de Mulhouse,
Oran (Tel. 353 66)

The following diving areas are popular with local SCUBA enthusiasts and visitors.

1. *Algiers Reghaia*   Small village 19 miles from Algiers. Deeps from 2 to 20 metres, 1 km from the shore; huge rocky blocks. Great variety of fish: muraenas, hogfish, mullets, squills, etc. Famous area for sprees and small tuna.

109

Alma Marine   36 miles from Algiers. Interesting area for beginners. Deeps of 2 to 12 metres. Small groupers, congers, hogfish.
Chenoua   62 miles from Algiers; easy access (1 mile from the beach) Deeps 6 to 20 metres. Groupers.

2. WEST OF ALGIERS

Damous   148 miles from Algiers. Groupers, giltheads, "chelbas", big red mullets etc. West of the beach near reefs accessible only by swimming. Camping facilities.

3. EAST OF ALGIERS

Dellys   134 miles from Algiers. Fishing 150 metres from the shore. Interesting area. All kinds of fish.

Between Dellys and Tizzirt   Fishing possibilities along a 15 mile coastline. Rocky creeks. Congers, muraenas, and above-mentioned varieties. Camping site.

Port-Gueydon   112 miles from Algiers. Rocky bottom about 2 miles from the shore. Great variety of fish. Camping site.

El Aouana Bay   Near Bejaia harbour. 187 miles from Algiers; very good road.

1—Les Aftis   About 6 miles before reaching El Aouana. Rocky bottom. Groupers, squills, etc.

2—Andreux Farm   5 miles from El Aouana. Beautiful creek, small forest and beach. Good camping site. Beautiful underwater landscapes. Small islet 500 yards from the beach. Very interesting area for exploration and camping.

Collo-Tamanar.   About 250 miles East of Algiers, towards Annaba. Ideal spot; rocky deeps 3 to 20 metres. Difficult access. Small boat necessary. Camping facilities.

Spear-Fishing

The use of air for spear fishing is generally banned, although the local *circonscription maritime* (Maritime Department) can grant special permission for cylinders to be used under certain circumstances. Exactly what these circumstances might be seems rather uncertain although, I can hazard a rather uncharitable guess! Providing you belong to a recognised diving or spear-fishing club no permission for snorkel spear-fishing is required. Divers without this qualification should apply to the local marine department for a permit. Advice about this can be obtained from the sub-aqua organisations listed above.

Further travel information may be obtained from: Algerian National Tourist Office, Time-Life Building, 153 New Bond Street, London W.1. (Tel: 01–493–7494/3144).

NOTE: A useful publication for anybody intending to explore Algeria is the guide in the well known Nagel series. This has maps, plans and a vast amount of detailed information including useful addresses and telephone numbers. The book can be obtained through the tourist office or from Nagel Publishers, Geneva.

AUSTRALIA

If you get the chance to dive off Australia you will have a unique opportunity of exploring vast areas of undived, virgin seascape. Breathtaking marine life, many of the species totally unafraid of the diver, and stunningly beautiful sub-aqua scenery combine to make Australian diving the experience of a lifetime. Facilities for the hire of equipment and cylinder filling stations are excellent although many of the best, unexplored, areas tend to be inaccessible except by boat or four-wheel drive vehicle so a well mounted expedition may be necessary. In the space available I can do no more than sketch in, region by region, some of the major places of interest. More detailed information can be obtained by contacting one of the underwater clubs or federations listed.

New South Wales

Diving is enjoyable all the year around, especially on the Northern coastline. It is an extremely popular area with divers and provides varied and interesting marine life, although around the major coastal towns some territorial species (i.e. Grouper) have been depleted by spearfishermen. Currarong, the Northern head of Jervis Bay and the Bay itself are prime diving areas. Further south Montague Island off Narooma is excellent for fish watching between December and April when warm tropical currents attract numerous species. In aptly named Disaster Bay there are numerous wrecks. To the north of Sydney, at Broken Bay, is the Bouddi National Marine Park. Off Smoky Cape you can see large grouper, specimens up to 500 lbs have been caught. A fascinating, but hazardous, dive can be attempted at Fish Rock an island about one mile off shore. Here a submarine cave bisects the island. It is possible to enter at one end in 35 feet of water and emerge 100 feet deep at the other side of the island. Several species are now protected, amongst them crayfish (may only be taken by hand on a snorkel dive), Abalone, Blue Grouper and Giant Cod. There are numerous clubs, hire shops and filling stations in this region. Clubs in the Sydney area can be contacted through Laurie Gaudry, 32 Hamilton Avenue, Earlwood. In the south contact Paul Jones, 60 Crown Street, Woollongong, in the north, Max Hazlett, 8 Bay Road, Terrigal. For full information contact the Australian Underwater Federation, 24 Victoria Street, New Lambton, N.S.W. 2305.

Northern Territory

The best diving months are September and October. There is a filling station at the Darwin Sub Aqua Club, PO Box 1850, Darwin 5794. (Tel: 852831). Diving along much of the coast is restricted to a few days each month because of poor visibility and strong currents. Careful study of charts and a good knowledge of the area is essential. There are a number of interesting World War II wrecks in the area. Further details may be obtained from the Darwin Sub Aqua Club of the Northern Territory Skindiving Federation of Australia, PO Box 1048, Darwin 5794 (Tel: 813375).

Queensland

All the year around diving with excellent facilities. Cook Island is a popular diving spot where you can find blue grouper, kingfisher surgeon, bream and forty-one other species. A boat is necessary. There are numerous reefs, for example off Gold Coast and Brisbane, many can be reached by snorkel from the beach. One kilometre north of Cowan Cowan is an astonishing artificial reef composed of wrecks ranging from whale-chasers and cargo boats to old cars! Stone fish are found in this area (see previous chapter) so great care is necessary. Other interesting diving areas include Old Woman Island, Double Island Point, Heron Island (a coral cay on the Great Barrier Reef) and Rockhampton. Certain species are protected by State Law or by private agreement amongst Australian divers. Contact the Queensland Underwater Federation, PO Box 651, Bundaberg, 4670, or the Queensland Government Tourist Bureau, PO Box 328,L Brisbane, Qld. 4001.

South Australia

Diving between late October and mid-April. Diving gear can be hired at repaired at the Adelaide Skin Diving Centre, 7 Crompton Street, Adelaide. There are few wrecks but abundant fish life. Contact the Adelaide Skin Diving Centre, at the above adress, for further information.

Victoria

Although the underwater landscape is not as awe-inspiring in this area as in others, abundant marine life and clean waters make for pleasurable and memorable dives. The best months for diving in this area are between November and May. There is a branch of the British Sub Aqua Club at Victoria. The Hon. Secretary is Mr A. Wood and the branch is the Frankston BSA 548. Their address is 30 Sintonia Road, Noble Park 3174, Victoria. You may also obtain help and information from the Australian Underwater Federation P.O. Box 56, Hampton, Victoria.

Melbourne is well catered for by a number of dive shops which will hire equipment and supply air.

The author during an expedition off Turkey. Note the special lens fitting on the underwater camera which is discussed in detail in chapter six. (See chapter six)

The problems of composition when using a frame finder are illustrated by these two shots. Although the diver appeared to be correctly framed, when the shutter release was pressed the difference in viewpoint between lens and finder caused him to vanish off the top of the picture. (See chapter five)

A diver exploring the wreck of a cargo vessel in the Mediterranean. (See chapter seven)

Associated Diving Industries, (Frankston/Melbourne) 8 Fenton Cr. (Tel: 783 7099). Will sell and service equipment, test bottles, supply air and offer diving instruction. These services are also available from Australian Divers (Spiro), 170 Abbotsford St. (Tel: MELB 30–4040) (Melborne North). The sales manager is Rod Dickson. The Southern Aquanauts Diving Academy at 21 Vale St. (Tel: 47 7535) (Reservoir/Melbourne) offers air and instruction. Other dive shops in the area are:

Australian Underwater Centre; 28 Howson (Tel: 50 3171) (Armadale/Melbourne). Hoath's Cycle 2 Sport Store; 529 Station (Tel: 893687) (Box Hill/Melbourne). Ski-Hire Pty Ltd; 23 Carrington Rd. (Tel: 89 5914) (Box Hill/Melbourne). Robinson Crusoe; 124 Prospect Hill Rd. (Tel: 83–3980) (Canterbury/Melbourne). Undersea Enterprises; 95 McDonald (Tel: 90–2224) (Mordialloc/Melbourne). Airdive Equipment Pty Ltd, 438 High Street (Tel: 51 5335) (Prahran/Melbourne). Ireland Ern; Vista Crt. (Tel: 870–6110) (Ringwood/Melbourne). Prahran Firearms Co. Pty Ltd; 171 Chapel (Tel: 51–6403) (Windsor/Melbourne). Scuba Diving and Marine Supplies Pty Ltd; 437 Spencer (Tel: 329–955) (Mel'bn).

Western Australia
On the Southern Coast dive between September and April, on the Western Coast from May to September. There are good facilities in this region. The area is rich in marine life and there are nearly 500 wrecks to explore. Both marine life and some wreck sites are protected under State laws. The west coastline at Eucla on the south to Esperance is unchartered and untouched. Red limestone cliffs fall to the sea. A four-wheel drive vehicle is essential for exploring this area. Cape Leeuwin, the southern most portion of the West Australian coast is the mecca for skin-divers but difficult currents and heavy seas make it an area for the experienced only. Other good areas include Denmark, William Bay, Peaceful Bay and Boat Harbour. A boat and a seaman with good local knowledge are essential for most worthwhile dives in this region. If possible dive at Carbadman Passage where the water drops off a reef to 600 feet and there is a fantastic amount of marine life. Northwards from Port Headland the coastline is almost deserted and little dived. Heavy tides make the area difficult and dangerous. Contact Council of Underwater Activities of W.A. Box T 1789 GPO. Perth 6001 (Tel: 266876 or 981876) Air is available at Port Headland, Esperance, Perth, Fremantle, Derby, Broome, Roebourne, Onslow and seven other towns.

For further information about visiting Australia contact the Australian Tourist Commission, 49 Old Bond Street, London W1X 4PL. Tel: 01–499–2247.

BALERIC ISLANDS

The three islands of Mallorca, Menorca and Cabrera off the Spanish coast are extremely popular tourist traps, especially Mallorca. Menorca is the least developed of the group and its coasline with more than one hundred beaches offers a wide variety of interesting dives. Marine life is plentiful; you can find bream, mullet, grouper, scorpion fish, cuckoo and peacock wrass, sting-ray, conger, octopus and squid. There are breathtakingly beautiful coral grottos and remote coves. There is much to interest the archaeologist as the remains of vessels dating from the Roman period lie around the shores. Very few of the more modern wrecks can be reached by shore dives and a diving boat is necessary. There are no tides and negligible currents with visibility of between 60 and 100 feet. In summer the water temperature rises to 80°F. Conditions are safe for the relatively inexperienced diver with easy access from the beach to depths of between 10–30 metres.

Excavation of wreck sites is prohibited without special permission and the removal of any marine life forbidden under strict local laws. It is easy to hire equipment and obtain air providing one has a Spanish diving permit. This may be obtained without difficulty by any diver who can show proof of competence to BSAC 3rd class standard or equivalent.

The oldest established commercial diving organisation on the island is Aquasport Menorca. Their office address is 54 Anden de los Martires del Atlante, Puerto Mahon. (Tel: 35 15 95). The man in charge of diving is Guy Webb. If you have made your own way to Menorca and want to dive, these are the people to contact. They also run inclusive diving holidays with air fares, hotel or apartment accommodation and twelve guaranteed dives. Further information about these package holidays can be obtained from Subaquasport Menorca, 122 Chancery Lane, London WC2A 1PP. Further diving and general information may be obtained from the Spanish National Tourist Office (see Spain).

BERMUDA

The Bermudas are a group of islands, all linked by causeways, in the Atlantic about 580 miles by South from Cape Hatteras on the American coast. Bermuda is about twenty-two miles long and about two miles wide. A fascinating and still largely undiscovered holiday spot both above and below the water. The winding roads are flanked by nibiscus and oleander, the pastel coloured houses have deep borders of white Bermuda Easter lilies, and chameleon-like lizards brood on gnarled cedar boughs. The water around these islands and islets are the clearest in the Western Atlantic since the position of the dotted landmasses enable them to escape the currents which stir up sediment. The average water temperature is 62 °F between spring and autumn. There are coral reefs and extensive marine life. SCUBA divers are well catered for on the islands, with a number of firms offering underwater safaris for those seeking organised dives. There is a sub-aqua club which will answer any queries visitors may have. The chairman is Bob Davey and the Secretary is Miss Wendy Smith. Their address is: Bermuda Sub Aqua Club, P.O. Box 521, Devonshire 4, Bermuda.

There are extensive wrecks around Bermuda, hardly surprising perhaps when one remembers the islands position and long seafaring tradition. Many of these wrecks are of great archaeological interest and are protected by law. Many are the remains of treasure ships and considerable fortune still awaits lucky divers on the reefs.

Visiting divers may bring in their personal SCUBA equipment free of duty. This includes normal items like cylinders, regulators, weight belts and so on. However, specialised gear which is only going to be brought in by serious treasure seekers may be subject to duty unless the diver has a special permit.

For the sport divers there are few restrictions in most of the sea areas, and anybody is free to dive on unprotected wrecks. However, some wrecks have been given legal protection and may only be dived by licensed divers. If you are interested in a particular wreck, you should contact the Receiver of Wrecks to discover whether or not your find has been registered and protected.

If you go to Bermuda with the specific intention of looking for treasure you must obtain a permit in advance of your trip from the Receiver of Wrecks. At the time of writing he is Mr K. R. Harding, Customs Department, Front Street, Hamilton 5–23, Bermuda. Such a licence is only granted providing you have permission for your visit as the issue of a licence is considered a form of employment, from the Immigration authorities. In fact licences are rarely granted to non-Bermudans and most casual divers would be put off by the amount of red-tape to be cut through. It must be emphasised, though, that these problems apply only to professional expeditions whose intention is to try and make their fortunes from diving around the islands. Ordinary sports divers have no need for permits.

Since there are such a number of wrecks, it may well be that the sports diver will come across a valuable find. The procedure is then as outlined in Chapter Seven of this book. The discovery must be reported to the Receiver. If the wreck contains treasure the Receiver will appoint an independent authority, the Smithsonian Institute, to value it. The Bermuda Government may then offer to buy the treasure at this valuation or allow the finder to keep it. This applies only to treasure located on unknown and, therefore, unregistered wrecks.

The following firms organise dives or hire equipment on Bermuda.

David McLeod Diving School
Operates March–November. (Tel: 1–6207)
1. *Scuba Dive to West Breakers:* for experienced divers. Depth: 40′ from "Seeker I" or "Seeker II". With scuba gear. 2 hours— $20.00.
1. *Scuba Dive to Wreck "Marie Celeste":* for experienced divers. Depth: 60′ from "Seeker I" or"Seeker II". With scuba gear. 2 hours— $20.00. Divers with their own equipment allowed $5.00 reduction on all dives.

	Months/ Hours	Price per Person
Underwater Safaris, Kevin Burke, Sonesta Beach Hotel Phone: 8–8122 etx. 217	All Year 9.00 a.m.– 6.00 p.m.	
3. *Scuba Dive*: dive to depths up to 40′ to reefs off the South Shore, from 27′ glass bottom boat "Shag"	1 hour	$20.00
4. *Combination of Nos. 1 & 2*	1 hour	$25.00
5. *Scuba Dive to Wreck:* depth 50′ from 27′ "Shag" With Scuba gear	1 hour	$20.00

Scuba Equipment Rentals
Masks, snorkels—fins, weight belts, air tanks, etc., are sold in sporting goods stores. The following places rent some equipment to visitors:

Harrington Sound Marina Smith's Parish, Phone: 3–0702	Mask, fins, snorkel	$3.50 per day (deposit $5.00)
	Mask, fins, snorkel	$2.00 half day (deposit $5.00)
Sportsman's Shop Reid Street, City of Hamilton Phone: 2–6024	Mask, fins, snorkel	$3.50 per day (deposit $10.00)
	Mask, fins, snorkel	$15.00 per week (deposit $10.00)
Bermuda Industrial Gases Boaz Island Sandy's Parish Phone: 4–1842	72 cft. tank	$3.00 per day (deposit $25.00)
	Air refill	$2.00 per day
	Back-pack	$2.00 per day

(Deposits are refundable)

NOTE: Visitors may rent a regulator from a licenced guide, providing he/she is accompanied on the dive by the guide.

Regulators are not rented to anyone who plans to dive alone.

Spear fishing is limited by Bermuda law as follows:
1. No spear fishing whatsoever is permitted within one mile of any shore. A diving lung may *NOT* be used.
2. A spear gun may *NOT* be used at any time. Under the regulations, "Spear Gun" means any weapon, apparatus or mechanism(s) constructed as to be capable of being used underwater for the discharge, whether complete or partial, or any projectile, whether or not a spear or harpoon.
3. No more than two fish of any one description, and no more than three lobsters may be taken in one day. *Lobsters may not be taken at all from April 15–September 15.*

There is at present no recompression chamber on the island, although efforts are being made to raise money to instal one at the Kind Edward VII Memorial Hospital.

For general information about the islands, travel and costs, etc. contact: Bermuda Department of Tourism, Trevor House, 58 Grosvenor Street, London W1X 0J0, (Tel: 01–499–1777).

FRANCE

As one might expect of the nation which more or less gave birth to the sport, and has produced some of the world's greatest divers, skin-diving is extremely well organised and popular in France. There are some 43,000 registered divers belonging to 580 clubs, organised under the Fédération Francaise d'Etudes et de Sports Sous-Marin (FFESSM). This Federation played an important role in the setting up of the World Underwater Committee in 1959. This Committee plays a major part in controlling and organising world wide diving. Each year the FFESSM publishes a diving guide which is a mine of information for any visiting divers. It lists all the clubs in the Federation and includes details of the equipment they possess, including recompression chambers, boats and so on. It also details the accommodation, camping sites and organise the hotels. This publication, which is in French, costs 20 francs and is well worth the money. It can be obtained from the FFESSM at 24 Quai de Rive-Neuve 13-Marseille. They are also willing to provide specific information about some particular diving area for example, providing you enclose an International Reply Coupon (you can get these at any Post Office) to cover the cost of their postage. The French Government Tourist Office, 178 Piccadilly, London W.1. (Tel: 01–493–3171) is also extremely helpful about general problems and queries connected with any visit to France, although their knowledge of diving matters is limited and they will probably refer you to the FFESSM. If you encounter any problems whilst in France it is possible to telephone the Federation for assistance. Their number is Marseille 33.99.31.

France has an immense and extremely varied coastline offering all types of diving. A party travelling by car can cross the Channel fairly cheaply and take all their own equipment with them, thus cutting hire costs. It takes about twelve hours fairly hard driving to reach the Mediterranean from one of the Northern ports and toll charges on the very fast auto-routes are high. When diving in an area it is advisable to contact the local club as they will be able to provide information about any possible hazards, tides and so on. Below I have listed the names, addresses and telephone numbers of thirty-three such clubs. In large towns and cities there may be half a dozen clubs and I have only included a few in each case. Most of these clubs are open for diving around the year and are very well equipped, they can supply air and most have their own recompression chambers. I have also listed the main equipment suppliers in France who may be able to help out if you lose or damage something vital.

NOTE: Under Paris I have listed the address only of probably the best known Club in France, the Club Méditerranée. This organisation runs all types of outdoor holidays in the sun.

1. *Aix-en-Provence*
   Groupement D'Explorations
   Et De Sauvetage Sous-
   Marins
   3 rue Entrecasteaux.

2. *Ajaccio* (Corsica)
   Sub-Aqua Club Ajaccio,
   6, rue Emmanuel Arene,
   (Tel: 21:00:20)

3. *Bastia* (Corsica)
   Cap Corse Club Sous-Marin
   Santa Maria di Lota, 20
   Miomo-Bastia.

4. *Biarritz*
   Biarritz Aquatique
   Scaphandre Club "Basc",
   6, rue du Bon air,
   Tel: 24.37.98
   Local: Port-Vieux et Port des
   Pêcheurs á Biarritz.

5. Groupe Subaquatique de
   Biarritz,
   5, rue du Heider.
   Tel: 24.37.19

6. *Bordeaux*
   Bordeaux Scaphandre Club,
   11, rue Gaston-Lespiault.
   Tel: 92.71.76, 92.91.75

7. Cercle Oceanaute de
   Bordeaux,
   38, cours Georges
   Clémenceau.
   Tel: 44.24.65

8. *Boulogne-sur-Mer*
   Club Sous-Marin de la Cote
   d'Opale,
   rue Amiral Bruix.
   Tel: 31.34.91

9. *Brest*
Groupe Manche Atlantique
de Plongée,
B.P.91.

10. Union Sportive de l'Arsenal
Maritime (U.S.A.M.),
groupe plongée,
DCAN, Port de Brest.
Tel: 80.10.00. poste 253

11. *Cannes*
Cannes Aéro-Sports,
section sports sous-marins,
Aérospatiale B.P.52.
06322 Cannes-La-Bocca

12. Club Alpin sous-marin,
10, place du Commandant-
Lamy,
Tel: 38.79.12

13. Club sous-marin de France,
2, rue Saint-Jin-Jin.
Tel: 38.13.22

14. *Dieppe*
Club des Sports sous-marins
Dieppois,
Arcade du Casino.
Tel: 84.28.67

15. *Dunkerque*
Club de plongée et
d'exploration sous-marines de
Dunkerque extensions,
C.P.E.S.M.D.E.,
64, quai des Hollandais.
Tel: 66.55.19

16. *Le Havre*
Club d'Explorations Sous-
Marines de la Manche,
(C.E.S.M.M.),
Sec. 100, bd. Francois ler.
Tel: (35) 42.79.61—42.46.78
—42.65.63

17. *Juan Les Pins*
Club International de
Plongée,
Club de la Mer,
Port Gallice.
Tel: 61.26.07 et 61.18.99

18. *Lyon*
Sub Aqua Gone,
35, Grande Rue de la Croix
Rousse.
Tel: 28.88.42

19. Union Rhodanienne de
Sauvetage et Recherches
subaquatiques,
92, rue Paul-Berg (3e).
Tel: Pt. 60.73.36

20. *Marseille*
Amicale Sportive Air-France,
Section pêche et sports sous-
marins,
41, La Canebière (ler).

21. Les Amis de la
Méditerranée,
Ecole de Plongée
Sur le Vieux-Port,
51, rue Gillibert (5e).
Tel: 48.36.67

22. Association des Amis
d'Archimè de,
116, cours Lieutaud (6e).
Tel: 48.79.48

23. Club sous-marin Provence
Côte d'Azur,
6, avenue des Lilas (9e).
Tel: 75.24.45

24. Cercle Subaquatique de Nice,
Luc Hôtel, place de la
Libération.
Tel: 84.98.54

25. Club des Explorateurs
Sous-Marins Nice Côte-
d'Azur,
34, av. de la Californie. Write
M. Segui, 46, rue Beaumont.
Nice. Tel: 89.10.59

26. La Plongée Nicoise,
20, rue Cassini.
Tel: 85.94.44

27. *Orleans*
Centre Subaquatique
Orleanais,
4, rue Daniel Jousee.
Tel: 62.21.65

28. *Paris*
Club Méditerranée,
Place de la Bourse (2e).
Tel: 742.09.09

29. *Saint-Jean-De-Luz*
Centre International de
Plongée Côte Basque,
30, rue Chauvin-Dragon.
Tel: 26.29.67

30. *Saint-Tropez*
Mer et Plongée,
Villa Lucie,
10, avenue Foch.

31. *Toulon*
A.S.S.P.T.
Association Sportive des
Sapeurs Pompiers,
Caserne des Sapeurs
Pompiers,
avenue Jean Moulin.
Tel: 41.58.24

32. Club Sub Aquatique
Toulousain,
20, place Wilson.

33. *Toulouse*
A.S.P.T.T. (Section chasse et
plongée sous-marine),
6, rue J. F. Kennedy,
Hotel des Postes.
Tel: 27.74.01

Diving Equipment Suppliers

Beuchat et Cie,
28, avenue Alexandre-Dumas, 13,
Marseille (8e).
Tel: 77.26.83 et 77.89.65.
President: Georges Beuchat.

Cavalero et Cie,
25, rue Gustave-Eiffel, 13,
Marseille (10e).
Tel: 48.29.20 et 48.26.28.
President: Rene Cavalero.

Christ,
Wet Suits,
Isocampe, 57, avenue de Verdun,
92 Chatillon.
Tel: 656.24.27

Comfort,
Ruelle des Moulins,
06 Nice.
Tel: (93) 89.63.30

Cressi,
38, rue Milton,
Paris (9e).
Tel: 878.87.70

Cristal,
40, rue des Bergers,
Paris (15e).
Tel: 250.83.17

Dimaphot,
16, rue Clément-Marot,
Paris (8e).
Tel: 225.14.86

Eumarcon
12, rue Rivarol, 30,
Nimes
and
50, rue Stendhai,
75 Paris (20e).

Europe Sport Diffusion,
nao socatex,
59, Forest-sur-Marque.

Exploration Sous-Marine,
3, rue Louis Astouin,
13002 Marseille.
Tel: (91) 90.67.03

Fenzy et Cie,
18, place de Villiers,
93 Montreuil.
Tel: 287.20.78

Les Hydronautes,
D. Mercier,
11, avenue de L'Estérel,
06160 Juan-les-Pins.
Tel: 61.23.13

Jopen,
103–105, rue du Berceau,
13 Marseille (5e).

Mossé,
71, rue Saint-Férreol,
13 Marseille (6e).
Tel: 33.34.15

Piel,
(Societe Industrielle des
Establissements Piel—S.I.D.E.P.)
16, rue des Belles-Croix,
91, Etampes.
Tel: 392

Ruggieri,
21, rue Ballu,
Paris (9e).

Scubapro-Euope,
8, rue Chabrier,
06300, Nice.
Tel: (93) 89.56.48

Sfacem,
34, rue Ribotti,
06, Nice.

Star France,
Societe d'Exploitation des
Etablissements Star France,
26, rue de l'Avenir,
66, Perpignan.
Tel: 34.63.78
Director: A. Bonneau.

La Spirotechnique S.A.,
Director M. Gaston Fournier,
114, rue Marius-Aufan,
92, Levallois.
Tel: 270.25.55

Sporasub,
93–99, ch. de la Mûre,
13, Marseille (15e),
M. Buffa.
Tel: 60.81.84

Squale Sport,
83, Sanary-s-Mer.
Tel: 336

You can dive off the Greek Islands more or less any time of the year as the sea and air temperatures remain mild. Summers are very hot and rainless so clarity is usually excellent, visibility up to 200 feet. There is a wide variety of marine life and many interesting wrecks on which to dive, although large numbers of them are protected as historic sites. The fish life includes grey and red Mullet, Blacktail, Swordfish, Gudgeon, Bass, Pike, Sole and Lamprey. Spear-fishing is prohibited within a hundred yards of any public beaches and in areas designated as nursery zones. Information on this subject can be obtained from: The Greek Amateur Fishing and Underwater Activities Federation, 4 Stadiou Street, 4th Floor, Athens (Tel: 3227–976) or the local harbour authorities.

Because of the valuable archaeological sites, diving may be prohibited in certain areas. Any enquiries regarding historic wrecks should be sent to: The Department of Antiquities and Restoration, 14 Aristidou Street, Athens (Tel: Athens 324 3056). Diving is permitted in the following areas:

IONIAN ISLANDS

Kerkyra (Corfu): Anywhere except the islands of Vido and Lasaretto, the area between Agni Cape and Aghia Ekaterini of Couloura, in the triangle between Mandraki, the northern part of Taxiarchis (Falacron), the southern part of Drasti and in the southern part of Lefkimi (from Arkoudila to Courdouri).
Paxi: Anywhere, except Voutsi area. *Lefkas. Kefallinia*: except in the Gulf of Sami and up to Aghia Efthimia. *Zakinthos*
Chalkidiki Peninsula
Cyclades Islands: ONLY in Mykonos
Argosarchikos Islands: Hydra, Spetse and Hermionis coast (Porto Cheli) In the above areas, underwater activities are subject to the control of the Archaeological Service who may forbid these activities to take place in areas where ancient remains lie.

Diving is prohibited in the following areas:
Kassandra Penisula Skioni, Sani, Mendi (Kalandra), Athitos Village up to Kallithea.
Sidonia Peninsula Kalyvia (ancient Mikiverna); Pyrgadikia (Ammos); Toroni (the community of Sykia coast); Porto-Koufo Port.
Mt. Athos Peninsula Duranoupolis and Ammouliani island; Olympias beaches (ancient Stagira)

In the event of an accident requiring re-compression, a chamber is available at the Naval Hospital of Piraeous, at the Federation of

Underwater Activities and at the Koulia School in Rhodes.

Sharks are only occasionally encountered, although some of the marine life can cause injuries and should be avoided (see Chapter Nine). Surface currents are found in the Corinth Canal, in Artemision, Argolio Gulf, Rion, Antirrion and in the Evripus Canal. Surface currents in the Aegean Sea do not exceed 3 miles per hour.

Prohibitions

The use of a breathing apparatus is only allowed in the areas permitted by the Archaeological Council. (By breathing apparatus it is meant all apparatus allowing a diver to remain underwater beyond the physical time limit) e.g. compressed air bottles, oxygen bottles.

The use of air-pump from boats is forbidden for underwater activities.

Spear-fishing species weighing under 150 grs. is forbidden as is selling of catches.

Spear-fishing is not permitted in ports near beaches and generally in bathing resorts. Persons under 18 years of age are not allowed to spear-fish.

Organised boat dives are available through Economy Holidays, 18 Panepistimiou (University) Street, Athens. Postal Address P.O. Box 581—Athens (Tel: 634–045 and 638–033). They will only take out divers who can show proof of having completed a third class diving course. There are reductions for groups and the diving boats may be chartered for as long as required providing advance notice is given. The normal operating months are between April and October but boats can be hired outside this period by prior arrangements. The company runs a 52 foot motor yacht the *Tamesis* which was built in 1965. She has six double cabins and two lounge cabins. One day cruises, which include meals, equipment and air, an English speaking dive leader, and two dives, cost around £10. The motor yacht leaves Athens every Saturday, Sunday, Monday and Tuesday at 9.30.

Independent divers can obtain air from the following centres:

Athens
Vouliagmeni Nautical Club.
Voula Nautical Club.
Kelamaki Nautical Club.
Hellinikon Nautical Club.
Old Phaleron Nautical Club.
Tzitzifies—Kallithea Nautical Club.
Club "Filon Aktis" 7 Karageorgi Servias Street.
"Nireus" Nautical Club of Argyra Akti, Nea Makri.

Pireaus
Piraeus Yachting Club.
Piraeus Club of Amateur Fishing, Passalimani.
Athens League of Amateur Fishing, Tourkolimano.

Eleusina
Eleusina-bay Nautical Club.

Lavrion
Lavrion League of Amateur Fishing.

123

Kalamata
Kalamata Nautical Club.

Central Greece
Katerini: Pieria League of Amateur Fishing.
Volos: Volos League of Amateur Fishing.
Lamia: Lamia Athletic Association of Amateur Fishing.
Lamia: Fthiotidos Union of Amateur Fishing, 20 Drossopoulou Street.
Halkis: Halkis League of Amateur Fishing.

Western Greece
Ioannina: Ioannina Nautical Club, 193 El. Venizelou Street, Ioannina.
Preveza: Preveza Nautical Club.

Northern Greece
Salonica: Union Of Amateur Fishermen.
Salonica: Yachting Club.
Kavala: League of Amateur Fishing.
Drama: Association of Amateur Fishing.

Islands
Crete: Heraklion Nautical Club.
Crete: Heraklion Union of Amateur Fishing.
Crete: Sitia Amateur Fishing Association.
Corfu: Corfu Nautical & Athletic Club.
Lesbos: Union of Amateur Fishing.
Hydra: League of Amateur Fishing.

General travel information can be obtained from: National Tourist Organisation of Greece, 195–197 Regent Street, London W1R 8DL (Tel: 01–734–5997)

ISRAEL

Diving is one of this country's fastest growing sports, and anybody who has had the pleasure in diving in their crystal clear waters will understand the attraction. You can dive in the Mediterranean, which forms the whole of the country's shoreline and in the Gulf of Eilat, which stretches from the town of Eilat to the southernmost tip of the Sinai peninsular. There is a wide variety of marine life and archaeological sites, caves and grottos to explore.

Diving is possible virtually all the year round in the Gulf of Eilat, except on the rare stormy days. The area is usually free of waves, currents are mild and tides moderate with variations of up to 80 centimetres ($2\frac{1}{2}$ ft.) between high and low tides. Visibility generally ranges from 15 to 40 metres (45–120 ft.) Water temperature ranges from 21° C (70°F) in February to 27°C (80°F) in August.

Most of the diving areas are close to the coast so that there is no need to use boats to reach deep water. Diving areas along the coast of Sinai can be reached by boats, cars or jeeps, and you will need to take along a portable compressor.

124

Fish, coral and sponges of every imaginable colour, shape and size inhabit these tropical waters. There are more than 100 different species of stone coral, and some dozen species of soft coral and sponges of which a few in each category are poisonous. Sea urchins, sea lillies, cucumber and starfish—about fifty species, crabs, shrimps, octopus and ink fish are among the main invertebrates to be found in the Gulf.

There are species of needle, pipe, trumpet fish, seahorses and others. Inhabiting the coral are five different species each of soldier, squirl, bat, angel fish, damesels and file fish; ten different kinds of surgeon fish; about fifteen kinds of butterfly fish and thirty of parrot fish, also a few dozen species of the wrasses family, twenty different varieties of cod, more than twenty-five varieties of groupers and various kinds of Moray eels.

Where the floor of the ocean is sandy, one can find, snappers, grunts, flatfish, twenty varieties of flounder and the venomous rabbitfish.

Among the other venomous fish are dragon, trigger, regal and common fire fish, crocodile fish, stone and scorpion fish. Less dangerous are the species of box, trunk, porcupine fish and puffers.

The deep open waters in relation to the reefs hold different species of flying fish, albacore, tuna, skipjack and twenty species of skate, ray, electric ray and manta ray. Among the predators are the common reef shark, sand shark, cat shark, thresher, whitetipper and hammerhead.

The taking of any species, living or dead, or any object from the sea or from the shore is strictly forbidden as the Gulf of Eilat is a Nature Reserve and its flora and fauna are protected by law.

The Mediterranean Sea
The Mediterranean has two good diving seasons—autumn (September to December) and spring (March to May), although there are also fine periods during the summer and winter when diving is possible. Visibility on good days averages 10 metres (33 ft.) with calm waters. Tides are never a problem as their average fluctuation is only 40 cms. (1½ ft.) even on rough days. Water temperature ranges from 16°C (61°F) in February to 29°C (84°F) in August.

Underwater Fishing
Underwater fishing is permitted at designated areas on the Gulf of Eilat, from Eilat to Ophira (Sharm-el-Sheikh) on the southern tip of Sinai. The whole of the rest of the Gulf is a Nature Reserve where underwater fishing is forbidden.

It is also permitted along the Mediterranean coast with the exception of the streches of coast between Ahziv and Rosh Hanikra and between Tantura and Habonim, those two stretches being Nature Reserves.

It should be noted that underwater fishing is permitted only with mask, snorkel and fins.

Divers are strongly advised to consult with local fishermen and divers as to the different types of fish and other marine life to be found at the stretch in which they are diving, since as stated, many of them are poisonous or, in other ways, dangerous.

Grotto and Cave Diving
Grotto and cave diving are possible at Rosh Hanikra, on the Mediterranean, in the north of Israel, and at various places along the Gulf of Eilat.

Divers are warned not to enter grottos or caves without an accompanying guide who is completely familiar with the region.

Underwater Photography
The cystal-clear waters of the Gulf of Eilat, with visibility of 40 metres (120 ft.) and even more make it a year-round photographer's paradise.

In the Mediterranean, with visibility up to 10 metres (33 ft.) photography is possible on all diving days.

Underwater Archaeology
The Mediterranean, cradle of ancient western and eastern civilisations, has a long maritime past. Trade by sea routes between the three continents—Europe, Africa and Asia—dates back to earliest history. This finds its expression in the many underwater ruins, wrecks and archaeological remains to be found on the bed of the Mediterranean.

Key areas of diving interest are to be found at: Phoenician Ahziv in the north; around the ancient harbour and fortress of Acre, Shikmona, south of Haifa; the Roman capital of Caesarea where part of the city is underwater; Appolonia, near Herzliya, where Pompey's fort has fallen into the sea; Palmachim, south of Rishon-le-Zion; and Ashkelon, where a forest of Roman columns lie like logs on the seabed.

Antiquities are also to be found in the Gulf of Eilat which is part of the ancient waterway between Asia and Africa.

Coins, pottery fragments, amphora, statues, weapons, shipwrecks, columns and much more are waiting to be discovered.

Archaeological finds are the property of the State of Israel and may not be removed from the site.

Information about archaeological diving can be obtained from: The Undersea Exploration Society of Israel, 21 Derekh Hativat Golani, P.O.B. 699, Haifa. Tel: 04–642345.

Facilities for Divers
Facilities for divers are provided by:

Aqua Sport, Red Sea Diving Centre Ltd.,
P.O.B. 300, Eilat.
Tel: 059–2788

Mediterranean Diving Center Ltd., Sidna Ali Beach,
P.O.B. 420, Herzliya Bet,
Tel: 03–937393 and 03–53584 (Diving Equipment Centre
14, Rehov Lilienblum, Tel Aviv).

The M.D.C. also has a base camp at Neviot (Nuweiba), Sinai,
75 kms from Eilat.

Organised groups of qualified divers can also receive services from:

Hugey Diving Tours,
Naama,
Ophira, Sinai.

Aqua Sport
The following services and facilities are provided by Aqua Sport:
1. Diving tours, for individuals and groups, to any point along the coast
of the Gulf of Eilat, using Landrovers and/or jeeps and carrying all
diving equipment and portable compressors. Overnights in tents. Tents
and sleeping bags for hire.
   Programmes can be worked out, in co-operation with travel agents,
on a package deal basis for country of origin. Land arrangements, which
are taken care of by travel agents, include accommodation and tours.
2. Diving School, in Eilat, recognised by the Federation for
Underwater Activities in Israel. Skin and SCUBA diving courses, from
the introductory to the advanced stages, and programmes for qualified
divers.
3. Rental and sale of diving equipment.
4. Air-filling services, spare parts and repairs, testing of cylinders and
calibration of instruments.
5. Guide for divers, groups or individuals.
6. Facilities for underwater photography; skin-divers can be
photographed by the Centre's underwater photographer. Developing
and printing service for black and white film.
7. Repair and maintenance workshops.
8. Life-saving equipment.
9. Equipment for the inspection of diving apparatus.
10. Technical library.

Mediterranean Diving Center Ltd.
The following services and facilities are provided by the M.D.C.
1. Diving tours for individuals or groups along the Mediterranean or
Gulf of Eilat. On tours of the Gulf of Eilat, overnights are spent in the
base camp of Neviot. (75 kms south of Eilat) in air-conditioned cabins
with showers.

127

Rates for Hire of Equipment from Aqua Sport

Per Day	1L	Per Day	1L
Mask	3	Weightbelt	3
Fins	3	Camera	30
Snorkel	1	Depth-gauge	4
Bathing suit	2	Movie camera	35
Diver's knife	3	Motor boat (1 tank)	100
Underwater torch (Batteries extra)	4	Landrover	75
Portable compressor	50	Tent and sleeping bag	5

7 litre single SCUBA (first fill)	18
10 litre single SCUBA (first fill)	20
14 litre double SCUBA (first fill) including regulator	25
Air filling service for all types of apparatus, 225 A.T.M.	6–8

All prices subject to change.
Night diving must be booked in advance.
Aqua Sport is open daily from 8.30 a.m. to 6 p.m.

Rates for Hire of Equipment from Mediterranean Diving Center Ltd.

Per Day	1L	Per Day	1L
Mask	3	Single tank (12-litre)	12
Snorkel	1	Double tank (20-litre)	17
Fins	3	Regulators	8
Weightbelt	3	Airfill—single	4
Diver's knife	3	Airfill—double	6
Life vest	5	Motor boat	50
Underwater torch	4		per hour

All prices subject to change.
Both the centres at Herzliya and Neviot are open daily from 8 a.m. until 5 p.m.

Hire of skin-diving equipment along the coast of the Gulf of Eilat to Ophira (*Sharm-El-Sheikh*)

Skin-diving equipment (masks, snorkels and fins) can be obtained, on a rental basis, at the following places along the Gulf of Eilat—apart from Aqua Sport, the Mediterranean Diving Center and Hugey Diving Tours.

Nelsons Village, Taba (8 kms. from Eilat).
Jackson on the beach facing Coral Island (14 kms.).
Neviot (Nuweiba) (74 kms.).
Desert Inn Caravan Resort Village, Naama (Marsa-el-Et) Bay (241 kms.).

Divers attending a course on marine archaeology at Fort Bovisand study notes made underwater on a plastic sheet. These can be made up using matt plastic paper, such as Ozalid, and a plastic pencil (made by Liberta Imax Ltd) to write with. Note the camera fitted with a wide angle lens in a dome part being used by the diver on the left. (See chapter eight)

The plastic record pad (shown in picture forty) being used underwater off Plymouth to record details of cannon. (See chapter eight) (Photo: Jim Gill)

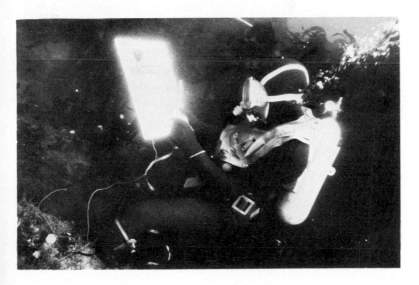

A diver checks an interesting stone with a clearly man-made hole in it. This might be an ancient anchor. (See chapter eight)

A survey instrument being used in the Mediterranean during experimental work. The optics have been specially designed to compensate for the effects of refraction. Diver-scientists like this man could soon be living and working for months on end under the sea. (See chapter twelve)

Programmes can be worked out, in co-operation with travel agents, on a package deal basis from country of origin. Land arrangements, which are taken care of by travel agents, include accommodation and tours. The Diving Centre usually supplements tour programmes with social activities such as kumsitz and fish-fry after diving.

2. Rental and sale of diving equipment—American, French and Italian.
3. Air-filling services, spare parts and repairs.
4. Diving School, recognised by the Federation for underwater Activities in Israel. The School offers diving courses, from the introductory to advanced stages, in any part of Israel or Sinai. It is mobile and prepared to move to wherever its services are required.
5. Portable compressors.
6. Motor boat.
7. Glass-bottomed boat (at Neviot).
8. Facilities for underwater photography.

Independent Diving Groups
Diving groups which are not taken care of by any of the aforementioned three bodies and which wish to dive outside the designated diving areas along the Gulf of Eilat—Deezahav (Dahab), Neviot (Nuweiba) and Naama (Marsa-el-Et)—must make arrangements for diving areas to be allocated to them, at least one month in advance, through: Local Authority for Sinai, Representative of the Ministry of Tourism, 9, Rehov Hataasiya, Tel Aviv, Tel: 03–35280 and 03–35291; or Local Authority for Sinai, Representative of the Ministry of Tourism, Ophira, Sinai, Tel: 057 99206.

The Federation for Underwater Activities in Israel
The Federation for Underwater Activities in Israel is a member of the international Underwater Confederation (C.M.A.S.). This body supervises all underwater activity—including safety standards and instruction—in Israel and Sinai and also supplies professional information on diving in Israel.

Address: 16 Rehov Hanatziv, Montefiore Quarter, Tel Aviv, Tel: 03–30841.

General tourist information can be obtained from the Israel Government Tourist Office, 59 St. James's Street, London SW1A 1LL (Tel: 01–493–2431).

KENYA

There is excellent diving to be had in the Indian Ocean, with calm seas and visibility in excess of 60 feet from October through to March. During the remaining months the seas are rough and visibility poor. There are many excellent diving areas, but most visitors will be limited to those areas adjacent to the three firms which organise expeditions and take out divers. The companies, listed below, provide all the necessary equipment but there are no facilities for independent divers to hire from them and then dive in unaccompanied groups.

The areas where dives are organised, however, provide the opportunity to observe a variety of coral and marine life of great beauty. Certainly every diver should aim to spend at least one holiday exploring the Indian Ocean, and Kenya makes an ideal base for such expeditions. There are no prohibitions on SCUBA diving, but spear-fishing with air is firmly discouraged by local divers who are naturally anxious not to have their fish massacred. There are only few shark sightings each year, Mike Warner, a professional diver who helps run Kenya Marina's, tells me that he only encounters sharks five or six time during hundreds of dives each year.

Diving groups with their own equipment can obtain air from the following sources:

Watamu Beach Hotel, Malindi (Tel: Watamu 1).
The Dolphin Hotel, Mtwapa area, some 15 miles north of Mombassa (Tel: Shanzu 232).
Kenya Marina's Ltd., Kikambala (Tel: Shanzu 208).
East African Oxygen, Mombassa.

The first three companies listed are the ones which organise diving expeditions, and should be contacted to make arrangements in advance of a visit. Their full postal addresses are as follows:

Watamu Beach Hotel, Box 300, Malindi.
Dolphin Hotel, Box 81443, Mombassa.
Kenya Marina's Limited, Box 15070, Kikambala, via Mombassa.

General tourist information can be obtained from most large travel agents or by writing to the Mombassa and Coast Tourist Association, P.O. Box 95072, Mombassa, Kenya (Tel: 25428).

LEBANON

With air temperatures above 70 °F from May to the end of October, good visibility and relatively unexplored waters along 180 miles of Mediterranean coastline, Lebanon has a great deal to offer visiting divers. East and West have met in this Middle Eastern country down the ages and there are important archaeological finds to be made around such historic international trading centres as Tripoli, Beirut and Byblos. In its history the Lebanon has been peopled by Phoenicians, Greeks, Romans, Byzantines, Arabs and Crusaders.

Diving is organised by the Subaqua-Club du Liban and the required visitors licence may be obtained through them. They can also supply air and hire all equipment. Their address is 727 rue Nahr, Guiliguian Building, Beirut (Tel: 232–606).

Many Lebanese learn to dive through courses run by the YMCA whose training methods are in line with those laid down by the BSAC. There is an organisation called the Dolphin Divers Academy which operates in conjunction with the YMCA and organises dives, but most Lebanese have a built in dislike of organised dives and prefer to form small, informal groups and arrange their own dives. If you go on your own to the Lebanon it is, therefore quite possible to meet up with local divers through the Subaqua-Club or the YMCA. Youth centres are run by the National Council of Tourism (Tel: 220–285) and they also provide accommodation at very low rates.

"Our visibility makes diving less interesting than other places in the Middle East" a Lebanese diver grumbled to me recently. However, since it can exceed 40 feet and is seldom worse than 20 feet, most northern water divers will happily accept these conditions.

A useful price saver for divers on a budget is the fact that you can set up camp anywhere you like in the Lebanon—although the tourist authorities suggest that the best camping is to be found at their organised sites—which means you can pitch your tent literally on the beach beside a favourite diving area.

You will need a visa to go to the Lebanon and these can be obtained either at Lebanese Embassies or Consulates abroad or at the frontier. Arab citizens do not need visas. You will also require an international vaccination certificate and, if you are driving, an International Driving Licence.

In the Lebanon help and advice can be obtained from the National Council of Tourism, Bank of Lebanon Street, Beirut (Tel: 340–940 343–175). In London contact the Lebanon Tourist and Information Office, Lebanese Embassy, 21 Kensington Palace Gardens, London W8 (Tel: 01–229–7265).

MALTA

As one who has enjoyed many memorable dives off this Island I can thoroughly recommend a visit. English is spoken throughout the Island, prices are reasonable and the climate first class during the summer months. Although very popular amongst tourists it is easy enough to find isolated bays where only a few locals ever seem to go. This may mean travelling over bad roads and then humping the equipment across country but the effort is well worthwhile. Visibility is excellent and there are few hazards, although beach dives may be a painful experience because of the sharp rocks and sea urchins. There are also interesting dives to be had off Gozo and Comino. A regular ferry service connects

Malta with these off-shore islands. It is possible to hire a local fishing boat quite cheaply to take you out to isolated bays. Off Comino there is a fine wreck close inshore. She is a coaster which appears to have run slap into the side of the island. Her fore-mast was still sticking up out of the sea on my last visit although the aft section lies in about thirty feet of water. Another well-dived wreck, now hardly more than a collection of steel plates, is the *Maori*, a World War II destroyer which was scuttled after being severely damaged by enemy action in 1941. You are quite likely to find the remains of Second War aircraft dotted around the coastline, there are at least three known Spitfires. There are also a number of sites of great archaeological interest and value. The lifting of artefacts is strictly prohibited needless to say.

Of equal interest to both the photographer and the sightseer, are the beautiful caves and natural features all around the island. There is an extensive and fascinating marine life; shoals of damsel fish and bogne, jelly fish and the giant pinna—a huge mussel-like creature can be found in certain regions.

All these and many others make Malta the ideal location for the fish reserve which has been suggested by Hans Hass.

Facilities

There are four branches of the BSAC and the MASC (Mediterranean Aquatic Sports Centres) located at the Villa Rosa Beach Club, St. George's Bay, has a complete Diving Sports Section. In association with Aquasports Limited, at the Tunny Net Restaurant, Mellueha Bay, they offer a wide range of underwater sporting facilities, including wreck hunting expeditions. The MASC Diving School have a training tank and a pool, and there is a large diving vessel available.

The oldest established diving centre in Malta is at Cresta Quay, St. George's Bay, St. Julians, where the diving is under the control of the Maltese Spear-fishing team of Edward Arrigo and Tony Micallef Borg. Cresta Quay, on the water's edge, is the meeting place of the Cresta Quay Special Branch of the BSAC. The Club can be visited on a daily basis.

All inclusive holidays are offered by Malta Diving Holidays, at Charles House in the town of Birzebuggia. This operation is run by Guy Webb and Vincent Milton, both BSAC members.

Cost of Equipment Hire (Approximate prices in U.K. currency)
1. *Cabin Cruiser carrying 10 persons*
£20 to £25 a day with skipper and diesel included. For an extra charge meals and drinks can be provided.
2. *Motor Launch* (with crew)
Maximum 30 persons   £30 daily
3. *Aqualung Diving*
Local Shore Dive   £2

Local boat or shore dive away from Centre   £2.25
Beginner with instruction
All equipment except wetsuit   £2.25

General details about travel and costs can be obtained from the Malta Government Tourist Board, 24 Haymarket, London SW1 4DJ (Tel: 01–930–9851).

NEW ZEALAND

Divers should contact the New Zealand Underwater Association for information and the addresses of Clubs in the areas they may be visiting. The address of the NZUA is 30 Orakei Road, Remuera, Auckland. No permits are required for skin-diving in New Zealand and there are no prohibitions on spear-fishing, although local divers have come to an agreement not to spear certain species around Poor Knights Island which is one of the finest diving areas. Visiting divers will certainly be made aware of this unofficial restriction and should abide by it. There are no wrecks of archaeological interest and modern wrecks may be difficult to locate without local guides. However, once divers come to know and trust you they are amongst the friendliest anywhere in the world and will be happy to make sure your visit is a memorable one. Water temperature varies in the north from 24°C in January, February and March to 14°C in July, August and September. The further south one goes the lower the temperatures become. The best diving in southern waters is to be had during the summer, whilst in Northland it is an all the year round sport most pleasant from November to June. The western coastline of New Zealand receives the prevailing winds and so the east has the calmest and clearest waters. Best diving off the South Island is to be found at either extremity. Poor Knights Island has been listed by the New Zealand magazine Skin-Diver in a short list of the world's finest diving locations.

Any divers contemplating a visit to New Zealand would do well to brush up their knowledge of the area by reading two first class books by that country's number one diver Wade Doak. *Beneath New Zealand Seas* is based on the author's experiences as a scientist/diver off Poor Knights Island and is a brilliantly illustrated introduction to the marine life of the area. The second book, based on practical observations over many years is *Fishes of the New Zealand Region*. These can be obtained from Wade Doak, Box 20, Whangarei, New Zealand.

Equipment Suppliers and Air
Diver Services (1973) Ltd., 73 Barry's Point Road, P.O. Box 30–113. Takapuna, Auckland (Tel: 494–806). Sales Director: Peter Fields.

133

This company hires all types of diving equipment including portable compressors and inflatables. They fill cylinders and service diving equipment. In addition they organise dives and run their own SCUBA school. Both Peter, and his director of underwater operations, John Ewen-Smith, are fully qualified divers with more than 30 years experience between them.

Another reliable supplier of hire equipment is:

Sportways, CNR Fort and Commerce Streets, Auckland (Tel: 379–502). Also at 27 Beach Road, Auckland (Tel: 372–316).

On South Island the best supplier is: Millners Underwater Centre, 126 Christchurch (Tel: 62–984). They fill cylinders and service equipment.

A convenient supplier for divers visiting Poor Knights Island is:

The Dive Shop, 19 Water Street, Whangarei, Northland (Tel: 83521). They hire equipment, fill tanks and arrange diving expeditions.

If you want to dive in comfort from the deck of a hired cruiser then contact skipper, Doug Schlegel on the "Lady Jess" (Tel: Ngungur 717), Write to RD3, Wrangarei, Northland.

Mayor Island, White Island, Mercury Island is the Bay of Plenty area. Divers operating in this area can hire equipment, get air and servicing of gear from: Tauranga Marine and Underwater Centre Ltd., 219 Cameron Road, Tauranga, (Tel: 83–757). (after normal working hours Tel: 89–469).

Information about travel to New Zealand and costs can be obtained from The New Zealand High Commission, New Zealand House, Haymarket, London SW1Y 4TQ (Tel: 01–930–8422).

SPAIN

The diver is extremely well catered for in Spain where skin-diving and particularly spear-fishing is a major sport. There are now regulations aimed at protecting some of the hard hit marine life which I detail below. A Spanish diving permit is necessary but this can be obtained by anybody who can prove his competence to BSAC 3rd Class Diver standard or the equivalent.

Air is available and equipment may be hired at most reasonable sized towns, close to the coast and the majority of large resorts or ports. The Spanish National Tourist Office in London can provide a map showing the location of sailing clubs and harbours which is an equally good guide to the location of diving facilities. The Spanish Federation of Fishing and Diving Clubs (Federacion Espanola de Pesca y Actividades Subacuaticas) is located at Escalinata 2, Madrid. Some of the more popular diving clubs are listed below:

Spanish Clubs

Centro de Recuperacion e Investigaciones Submarinas (C.R.I.S.) with offices in Barcelona, Provenza 284,3 has compressors at:
Barcelona, Rocafort 191; Blanes (Gerona), Pasco de la Maestranza 66, (Gerona), Medicos 8. It has decompression chamber in Barcelona, Rocafort 191.

Almenia—Section de Pesca Submarina y Escafandriamo del Club de Mar.

Cartagene—Decompression chamber at the Naval Base.

Ceuta—C.A.S.—Espin 16.

Denia (Alicante)—C.I.A.S.—Jose Antonic 28.

Luarca (Asturias)—Sociedad Deportiva Luarquesa.

Mataro (Barcelona)—S.P.A.S.—Ave. Generalisimo 46.

San Sebastian—A.P.S.A.S.—Ave. Generalisimo 22.

Santander—C.I.S.—Jardines de Pereda
     GRUNSANA—Pasajo del Arcillero 2,1
     Tiro Nacional S.A.S.—Promontorio de San Martin.

Tarragona—C.E.S. San Antonio 41.

Valencia—A.J.A.S.—Pascual Genis 20.
     C.I.A.S. Ave, Marques del Turin 12.

Underwater Holidays

Club Méditerranée,
40 Conduit Street, London W.1.

Club Rio Verde, Marbella, Spain	Have inclusive diving holidays in Spain, Italy, Sardinia and Turkey.
Club Poscidon Nimrod, Hotel Piccina Salvi, San Feliu de Guixols, Costa Brava, Spain.	For experienced divers only. Includes Diving expeditions off the North African coast.

Spear-fishing Regulations

1. Must only be undertaken for sport, catches may not be sold.
2. Divers, who must be over 18, require a permit issued by the Naval authorities in the area to be dived. These "Comandantes de Marina de las Provincias Maritimas" function under the direction of the Spanish Ministry of Commerce which introduced the regulations in 1966.
3. To obtain a permit, divers, or clubs, must apply giving the following information:
   a) Passport with visa (where necessary).
   b) Two passport sized photographs.
   c) Proof of membership of a recognised underwater club, proof of competence as a diver.

Divers who belong to the BSAC should have no trouble about

135

meeting these requirements. If you belong to a non-BSAC club then, providing it is properly organised and well established, you should still be able to obtain the permit.

4. Permits cover only the sea areas for which they are issued.

5. Underwater fishing is prohibited:
   a) From sunset to sunrise.
   b) Within 100 metres of fixed or floating nets and of fishing vessels engaged in their work.
   c) When using underwater lamps.
   d) With aqualung equipment of any type.
   e) With explosive powered harpoon guns.
   f) In special areas of prohibition.

It is also an offence to carry a cocked harpoon gun out of the water. A stiff fine is the penalty for any infringement of the regulations. Further information can be obtained from: Direccion General de Pesca, Subsecretaria de la Marina Mercante, Ministerio de Comercio, Madrid, and from the Spanish National Tourist Office, 70 Jermyn Street, London S.W.1. (Tel: 01–930–8578).

TURKEY

You can take your choice from the Black Sea, the Sea of Marmara, the Aegean Sea and the Mediterranean if you go diving in Turkey. Each area provides a wide range of interesting scenery and marine life. The summer weather is usually excellent with the two hottest months being July and August.

There are no prohibitions, except for safety reasons in certain areas, on small groups of sports divers, although the use of professional diving equipment is forbidden. Diving is under the control of local authorities in the areas listed below.

There is a large number of valuable wreck sites around the Turkish coast and diving on these may be subject to restrictions. The most ancient wreck ever discovered, a Bamza age relic of the Trojan wars, more than 32 centuries old, lies in the Mediterranean off Cape Gelidonya, for example.

Currents in certain areas can be dangerous and local advice should always be sought before starting to dive in an unfamiliar region. For boat dives Turkish fishing craft can be hired quite cheaply on a day to day basis.

Because of the difficulty in obtaining hire equipment, divers intending to explore Turkey would be well advised to travel down by car taking all the gear needed with them. Air, and some equipment, can be obtained from the following sources:

1. Turk Balak Adamlar Kulubu, Caddebostan—Istanbul, Tel: 55 56 28.
2. Karsiyaka Balik Adamlar Kulubu, Karsiyaka—Izmir.
3. Bodrum Balik Adamlar Kulubu, c/o Bodrum Turizm ve Tanitma Burosu Sefligi, Bodrum.

Local authorities controlling diving:
a) In Kara Ada Region (within the boundaries of the town of Bodrum) on the coastal strip between Baglar Burnu (Cape Baler) and Kisla Buku.
1. Latitude 36 ° 15 ' 45 "—Longitude 30 ° 47 ' 55 "
2. Latitude 36 ° 41 ' 22 "—Longitude 30 ° 24 ' 45 "
b) In the Bay of Antalya, the coastal strip between Babe Burnu (Cape Babe) and the rocks to the north of Av Burnu (Cape Av).
1. Latitude 36 ° 50 ' 45 "—Longitude 30 ° 47 ' 55 "
2. Latitude 36 ° 42 ' 22 "— Longitude 30 ° 34 ' 37 "
c) In the Bay of Marmaris, the coastal strip between Turunc Buku and Kutuk Brunu (Cape Kutuk)
1. Latitude 36 ° 48 ' 37 "—Longitude 28 ° 14 ' 15 "
2. Latitude 36 ° 48 ' 35 "—Longitude 28 ° 14 ' 40 "
3. Latitude 36 ° 48 ' 40 "—Longitude 28 ° 15 ' 35 "
4. Latitude 36 ° 40 ' 55 "—Longitude 28 ° 15 ' 55 "
d) In the Casme Region, the coastal strip to the east of Deniz Liman and Ilion.
1. Latitude 38 ° 20 ' 45 "—Longitude 26 ° 19 ' 30 "
2. Latitude 38 ° 18 ' 32 "—Longitude 26 ° 22 ' 15 "

Diving is not permitted in the following areas for safety reasons:
1. The area around the main quay in Marmaris harbour.
2. The area covered by a circle, the ardius of which is 900 m., with the lighthouse and the breakwater in Yesil Cukarli as the centre.

Members of organisations who arrive in Turkey in large groups to carry out underwater scientific experiments must apply for permission through the Foreign Office (Ministry of Foreign Affairs) in Turkey.

Divers arriving in Turkey by private boats must hire Turkish boats for diving and observe the rules laid down above.

Further information on travel may be obtained from The Turkish Tourism & Information Office, 49 Conduit Street, London WLR OEP (Tel: 01–734–8681/2).

YUGOSLAVIA

Diving in the clear, warm water of the Adriatic is an experience to be treasured and the coastline around Yugoslavia is one of the most beautiful in Europe. To avoid difficulties you must abide strictly by the

137

regulations controlling diving. Any underwater activity where air cylinders are used requires a diving permit from the security services responsible for that particular area. You will need to fill in an application form giving your name and address, the type of underwater activity you wish to follow, technical details of the equipment being used, the sea area where you propose to dive and the approximate time of your dives. When diving the area must be marked with a yellow spherical marker with a diameter of around 18 " placed in the centre of the diving zone. Diving in port areas, along navigational routes and in the vicinity of military installations is prohibited as is any diving within 900 yards of any warship. There are also some areas where even snorkel diving is forbidden. Although such zones are few you must ensure that you are not infringing any of the regulations. *Such prohibitions are not to be treated lightly*. Spear-fishing with air is forbidden.

If you join one of the Yugoslav diving or sports fishing associations, the annual membership fee is around £12, you will be given a membership card which serves as a diving permit all along the Adriatic. You will only be able to join these organisations if you can show membership of a similar fishing or diving club in the U.K. Even with this card it is advisable to contact the local tourist office in the area where you intend to dive. They will tell you of any prohibitions and whether it is necessary to report your presence to the local police. So long as you take these precautions there should be no problems. Fishing boats are available for hire either from local ports or from fishing associations. Diving gear can be hired and air obtained at the towns and resorts listed below.

To become a member of the Yugoslav Diving Association apply to one of the following organisations:

"Partizan" Physical Fitness Association Belgrade.
Underwater Sport Association of Zagreb.
Sea and Land Research Association, Ljubljana.
"Uljanik" Sport Fishing Association of Pula.
"Luben" Sport Fishing Association, Rijeka, or
"3 Maj" Sport Fishing Association of Rijeka.
"Kostrena" Sport Fishing Association, Kostrena.
"Pelagrin" Sport Fishing Association, Hvar.
"Kornatar" Sport Fishing Association, Murter.
Underwater Research Centre, Kostrena.

Air is obtainable to 150 ats at Piren, Losinj, Pula, Opatija, Rijeka, Sibenik, Hvar, Herceg-Novi and Belgrade.

Suggested diving areas
Zadar—northern Dalmatia, first settled several centuries B.C. Sandy beaches.

138

Biograd Na Moru—A small town on a peninsular surrounded by pine woods. Sandy beaches.

Primosten—A beautiful village on what was once an island, now connected to the mainland. Sand and rocky beaches.

Island of Krk—The largest Yugoslav island, connected to mainland by ferry. Sandy beaches.

Island of Lastovo—Wooded island, beaches of sand and shingle, olive groves and orchards.

Elafiti Islands—A string of islands off the Dubrovnik Riviera. Pine woods and rocky beaches.

All the areas listed above are noted for the richness of their marine life. If you come from Britain no visa is required and you can get a 30 day tourist permit at the frontier for a small fee. Further information may be obtained from: Yugoslav National Tourist Office, 143 Regent Street, London W1R 8AE (Tel: 01–734–5243).

Section Three

11

The Sea and the Challenge

There is a planet in our solar system whose deepest secrets remain undiscovered, two thirds of which is largely unexplored and about which we know less than the surface of the moon. That planet is earth.

Three-quarters of our world is covered by 139 million square miles of water to an average depth of nearly two and a half miles. Ninety-two million square miles of ocean are deeper that 600 feet and form the Abyss, not only the most secret region left on earth, but the most dangerous and challenging environment left for mankind to explore on this planet.

The Abyss has yielded few secrets so far to scientists who have dangled their electronic equipment in its depths, bounced sonar beams from the glutinous sediments which coat its valleys, or made brief and dangerous forays into its pitch black depths.

We do know that there are peaks higher than Everest in the Abyss, mountain ranges stretching for thousands of miles, and gorges deeper than the Grand Canyon. We know there are valley systems in the Abyss more extensive that the 3,700 mile length of the Mississippi and submarine "winds" which scour the submerged peaks. We know that the Abyss contains billions of living creatures ranging from giant squid to microscopic plankton, that there are fish which glow with their own bioluminescence and, blind fish which home on their prey by sonar systems, that there are flat fish which spend their entire lives in pitch blackness under a pressure of hundreds of tons per square inch.

The relatively shallow waters of the Coastal Shelf is where skin-divers spend their time, and provides much that is interesting in diving, from wrecks to easily observed fish, but it must be remembered that these waters, down to 600 feet, form only about 3 % of the total area of the oceans. Of the remainder approximately 80 % is more than 10,000 feet deep, whilst about 30 % is more than 13,000 feet deep. The deepest parts of the oceans are the plunging underwater canyons known as trenches. There are fourteen in the Pacific, the deepest being the Marianas Trench in the western Pacific at 36,200 feet. The Atlantic Ocean has two trenches of which the 30,184 feet deep Puerto Rico Trench is the deepest and there is one, the Java Trench, 24,442 feet deep, in the Indian Ocean.

The marine environment has been divided into three zones. The *Neritic region* contains all the water above the Continental Shelf, the *oceanic region* below the Continental Shelf and *the Abyss*. The shore too is zoned into the epilitoral, that part of the shoreline which is just within reach of sea spray but never engulfed, the culittoral zone, that part of the beach covered and uncovered by tides and between these zones is the sublittoral region.

It is the neritic zone about which we have the most knowledge, and in which the sport of skin-diving was born in the 1920's when an American author Guy Gilpatrick, turned a pair of old flying goggles into a crude diving mask.

Before turning our attention to this pioneer, and his adventures off Cap d'Antibes let us plunge off the Continental Shelf and down the Continental Slope into the Abyss to discover what sort of a world divers in the year 2000 will discover if advances in technology have enabled them to live and work at the furthest depths of the ocean.

The seascape of the Abyss is rugged and harsh, layers of sediment up to 40,000 feet thick coat the bottom. Sediment on the floor of the Pacific averages 1,000 feet, and in the Atlantic 2,000 feet. These enormous deposits are less surprising when we remember that each year the rivers and streams of earth carry some 3 billion tons of land out to sea. The Mississippi alone transports 750 million tons of the North American Continent into the Gulf of Mexico annually.

Perhaps one of the most astonishing features to confront the explorers of the Abyss will be flat topped mountains, named guyots after a 19th century geologist, Arnold Guyot. These are mountains whose peaks were erroded millions of years ago. Today guyots can be covered by as much as 6,000 feet of ocean, but dredging surveys have brought up pebbles from their plateaux rounded by surf. These are drowned islands upon whose beaches the tides rose and fell a 100 million years ago in the age of the dinosaurs. What sent them sliding into the depths of the Abyss? One theory is that the earth's crust was too weak to support the weight of these newly born mountains. As the centuries passed the sea encroached upon them more and more, wearing the peaks flat. Coral grew on the shallow, submerged areas until one day they plunged into the depths.

Some mountains of the Abyss still break the surface, the world's tallest mountain Mauna Kea (Mountain White) on the island of Hawaii rises 33,476 feet from the depths with only the last 13,796 feet above water. In the Mid-Atlantic ridge, the first submarine range to be mapped, during the laying of the earliest transatlantic cable in the 19th century, extends for more than 10,000 miles from Jan Mayen Island north of Iceland almost to the Antartic Continent. A few of the peaks thrust above the surface as the islands of St. Helena and the Azores but most are crowned beneath thousands of feet of ocean.

It was only during the intensive field work which took place during the International Geophysical Year in 1957, scientists realised that the Mid-Atlantic ridge joins others in the Indian Ocean and Pacific to form a

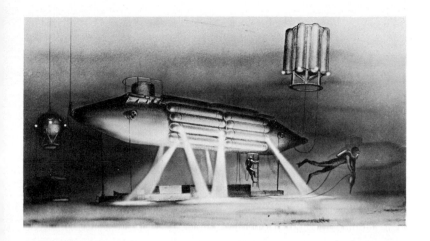

An artists impression of BACCHUS (B.A.C. Commercial Habitat Under the Sea) which was designed by the British Aircraft Corporation as an aid to research, exploration and salvage work. (See chapter twelve)

A crude but workable inflatible underwater house in Paradise Bay, off Malta. Set up by two London colleges in 1969 the house was used in underwater living experiments. A diver/scientist spent a week living and working in the habitat. On the right can be seen the special power pack which supplied light and life support power to the house which was anchored at 30 feet below the surface. (See chapter twelve)

Divers ferry scientific equipment in a pressurised steel case during underwater living experiments off Malta in 1969. (See chapter twelve)

A picture which symbolises man's twin exploration of outer and inner space. Skin-divers aid American astronauts during training in a giant tank—used to simulate weightlessness. But man's mastery of inner space, the oceans of the world, looks like proving even harder than the moon landing programme. (See chapter twelve) (Photo: USIS)

vast network of drowned peaks, the greatest and probably the oldest range of mountains on earth extending more than 40,000 miles in length with a width varying between 300 and 1,200 miles. The fact that man discovered this only twenty years ago gives some indication of our ignorance about the oceans.

Between the mountains and guyots there are deep valley systems, whose origin remains a mystery. Nobody has been able to explain what colossal activity was responsible, for example, for scouring the submerged valley that runs from the mouth of the Hudson river, This valley is 180 miles long and plunges to 14,000 feet below sea level, cutting a groove which is more than 4,000 feet below the ocean floor in places.

In 1960 during "Operation Nekton" the French aquanaut Jacques Piccard, with Lieutenant Donald Walsh of the American Navy, took the baythscaph Trieste down to 35,800 feet in the Marianas Trench. On the pitch black bottom, seven miles down, their spotlight swung slowly, a pinprick of brilliant light in the Abyss. Suddenly a living creature appeared, transfixed in their beam. The divers reported: "Slowly, very slowly, this fish, apparently of the sole family, about a foot long and half as wide, moved away from us, swimming half in the bottom ooze and disappeared into the black night, the eternal night which is its domain."

What sort of creatures live and breed in perpetual blackness where the pressure is nearly 300 tons per square inch and how can they exist? Taking the Abyss as starting at some 700 feet we know that the cod, and their close relative the "rat-tail" a fish, whose heavy body tapers rapidly to a fine membrane which gives the species its name, can be found at this depth and below. The cod makes forays into the Abyss, the rat-tail is one of the most common deep water fish. Its eyes are large and considered amongst the most sensitive in the animal kingdom enabling it to cope with the dim light of the depths. Even below 13,000 feet where no trace of daylight can penetrate, its uniquely sensitive eyes are useful, enabling it to detect the luminescence of other deep sea-creatures.

But other deep sea species, for example, the large headed Brotulids, have lost their sight completely. This was discovered when one was dredged up from the depth of more than 16,000 feet in the Celebes Sea. These and other species whose eyes have degenerated into near uselessness, make use of the lateral-line system, a method of detecting prey and predators which is unique to fishes. The lateral-line which can be seen quite clearly in some species, is made up of rows of highly sensitive cells along each side of the body which receive low-frequency sound waves. During one experiment, blinded fish were able to detect disturbances caused by agitating the water in an aquarium tank with a glass rod no thicker than a hair. The acoustic waves which stimulate these cells travel at 5,000 feet per second so this "sixth-sense" works at high speed. The lateral-line system can also be used as an underwater sonar. As the fish swims, movement of his body through the water creates shock waves. When these strike another object they are bounced

145

back and detected by the lateral-line cells. The fish can measure the time lag and thus sense how close he is to other marine creatures. Biologists believe that larger species of fish can detect their prey at a distance of more than 60 feet.

Although our explorers would be unable to hear the low frequency sounds which trigger a response in the lateral-line system, they would find the Abyss far from silent. Despite the fact that fish have no vocal chords the depths are alive with noises, ranging from deep siren sounds like off-key organ pipes through an acoustic kaleidoscope of shrieks, gurgles, grunts, whistles, clicks, booms, croaks, drummings, rattlings, honks, clunks and hissings.

These sounds all of which have some specific purpose, are made in two main ways. The swim-bladder, a hollow organ which helps maintain the fishes buoyancy, may be vibrated or parts of the horny skeleton may be rubbed together. Lobsters "call" by drumming their long antennae against their armour, whales and dophins use a high squeaking whistle to communicate, as any diver who has swum alongside these fascinating creatures can testify. In the depths it is thought that some of the sounds are part of a sonar of far greater range than the lateral-line system, to enable fish to orientate themselves with both the bottom and the sea surface. One set of signals, followed at regular intervals by a weaker note which was judged to be the echo of the fish's call bouncing off the seabed some five thousand feet below the creature, were detected by a survey ship at a depth of more that 11,000 feet.

No daylight can ever penetrate the icy darkness of the Abyss, but the visitors would still see glimmering lights in the eternal night. These are caused by the bioluminescence produced by certain fish. Commonly called phosphorescence the process has, in fact, nothing to do with phosphorus at all but depends on a complex reaction based on a chemical called "luciferin". One such luminous fish is Idiacanthus panamensis, an eel like creature, found during the day at a depth of 5,000 feet or more, which has light producing centres at the end of its barbels and on the body. Such lights may serve two purposes. Firstly simply to illuminate the Abyss, some fish seem to use especially powerful areas of luminescence on their bodies as spotlights which can be trained at will on the surrounding ocean, and secondly as a lure for food. One species of angler fish which lives on the ocean mud at depths down to 12,000 feet, uses a luminous bait placed between its cavernous jaws.

It was into this world, so alien to man, that Jacques Piccard and Donald Walsh dived on January 23rd, 1960. The descent began at 8.23 a.m. in rough weather which buffeted their bathyscaph Trieste heavily, as the towing lines to the U.S. Navy's ocean going tug Wandank were parted, some 200 miles off Guan in the western Pacific. Below their craft, seven miles down, lay the floor of the Mariana Trench. By the time they reached the bottom their bathysphere would be withstanding a pressure equal to the weight of five battleships. At 1306 the Trieste touched down on a uniform carpet of ivory coloured sediment. Don Walsh picked up the phone and called the Wandank with the historic news that man had reached the deepest part of the ocean. They stayed on the bottom for twenty minutes, took measurements of the temperature, undersea currents and looked for any indication of radio-activity. They observed the flat fish flapping its way through the ooze and saw a shrimp swim past their porthole. Then they ascended.

Behind Operation Nekton this significant plunge into the unknown, lay years of research and dives to lesser depths. Behind Piccard and Walsh the ghosts of other divers, the pioneers who had first opened up the depths for mankind. Centuries before any type of diving apparatus was invented men living around the warm waters of the Mediterranean and Pacific, had learned the art of free diving. By training from childhood they were able to reach enormous depths, down to 200 feet, where water pressure compressed their chests to the width of a man's thigh. They were able to hold their breath for well over two minutes, and carried out salvage as well as military operations. During the siege of Syracuse, the Sicilian capital, in 400 BC, divers were used to cut down underwater barriers which had been constructed to prevent Greek warships from entering the harbour, and accounts of similar operations at the siege of Tyre have been found.

Aristotle describes primitive breathing tubes, which allowed divers to spend prolonged periods underwater, and an account has been preserved of how Alexander the Great used a machine named Colimpa to descend underwater.

This may have been a similar type of diving-bell to one designed nearly two thousand years later by Dr Edmund Hailey in which descents were made to sixty feet or more. Attempts around the same period to construct a waterproof diving suit were less successful, but in 1715 a Devonshire inventor, John Lethbridge managed to design a "watertight" leather case for enclosing the person. The suit held air and was built to allow the diver to walk about on the bottom and salvage wrecks. Lethbridge is said to have made a fortune with his invention.

The 19th century, that great age of the inventor and explorer, saw a considerable development in underwater technology. In 1939 the world famous diving firm of Siebe, Gorman and Company were formed. Forty years later they produced the first independent diving equipment, which liberated explorers from the bondage of surface tubes and wires. This was a type of rebreathing apparatus similar in principle to that used by frogmen during the Second World War. Designed by Henry Fleuss, a merchant seaman, the diving equipment included a rubber face mask, which supplied air via flexible tubes from a copper cylinder containing oxygen under 30 atmospheres pressure and absorbed carbon dioxide with a pad of yarn soaked in caustic potash. Fleuss tested the equipment himself by dropping over the side of a rowing boat off the Isle of Wight. To make himself negatively buoyant this intrepid

147

Wiltshireman hung pieces of lead around his belt and strapped chains to his ankles. Not content with a straightforward experiment, the world's first free-lung diver switched off his oxygen supply twenty feet below the surface to see what would happen. He blacked out immediately and was hauled back into the boat as dead. He came around after a few moments however screaming in pain and vomiting blood. The rapid ascent as friends pulled him up on a safety line had saved his life but ruptured his lungs. A few weeks later he was diving again.

Fleuss was lucky, over the decades which followed many pioneers died but, little by little scientists like John Scott Haldane, and diving doctors like Dr Alphonse Gal, the first medical practitioner to study man underwater, came to understand the problems and dangers of diving. As the need for decompression stages became known deep dives became possible. In 1906 two volunteers, Petty Officer Andrew Catto and Lieutenant Guybon Damant, took part in experimental deep dives as part of a programme devised by Professor Haldane. In Lock Striven, Damant plunged 210 feet and surfaced unharmed. It was more than eight years before any diver equalled this feat.

Damant and Catto were hard helmet divers, breathing air supplied from a pump on the surface. With this vital breathing tube and the other lines to safeguard the hard-hat diver ran considerable risks when exploring or carrying out salvage work on wrecks. Nevertheless some remarkable feats of salvage were carried out, perhaps the most spectacular taking place off Malin Head, Donegal, during the First World War. In charge of operations was the indestructible Captain Damant.

During January, 1914 the White Star liner Laurentic, bound for Halifax from Liverpool, struck a mine and sank in 120 feet of Atlantic water. More than three hundred of her crew died, either during the sinking or from the exposure in the open lifeboats. The Laurentic had carried no passengers, but £5 million worth of gold bullion was stored in her second class baggage room, on its way to Canada to pay for war materials. Damant, now Lieutenant-Commander, and the most experienced salvage diver in the Royal Navy, was given the task of salvaging the gold bars.

At first, despite rough conditions in the area which lay exposed to northerly and westerly gales, it seemed as if the operation might be accomplished without too much difficulty. Six weeks after the sinking, Damant's reconnaisance diver was lowered into the vast hull of the wreck, which had keeled over at sixty degrees to port. So massive was the vessel that the depth from the suface to the upper deck was only sixty feet. The port cargo hatch was blown open and the first divers entered the wreck. They found passageways to the bullion store blocked by piles of loose stores, furniture and other debris which had be be dragged out of the way. Eventually they reached an iron-bar door leading to the baggage room passageway. This was blasted aside with explosives. Struggling deeper into the darkness of the wreck, diver E. C.

Miller finally reached the steel door of the baggage room itself. In total blackness, his hands numb from cold, Miller felt along the steel plates until he had located the massive hinges. Using a hammer and chisel he knocked the door open. Stumbling inside, his fingers made contact with a solid wall of gold bars, each ingot weighing 140 pounds. During the first week of operations more that £32,000 worth of gold was salvaged and Damant began to hope the operation might be rapidly concluded. Then a storm forced them back to harbour. With nothing else to do Damant took a stroll along the beach, and made a disturbing discovery. Amongst the wreckage washed ashore were scores of white tiles from the second class smoking room which was located amidships and three decks down. The conclusion was obvious. The Laurentic was breaking up fast.

When the weather eased they returned to the wreck site. This time the diver passed the sixty foot mark and kept on descending, his feet finding no supporting deck. The ship had collapsed in on herself and the passageway to the gold was now covered by tons of steel plate, twisted girders and broken machinery.

Damant went down to see for himself and decided that his divers would have to use explosives to tunnel their way towards the gold. As the charges went off trapped corpses floated free from the wreckage and provided a banquet for the sharks which gathered in their dozens around the diving tender.

Finally they reached the baggage room at a depth of 120 feet. The gold had gone, scattered amongst the wreckage. Damant recalled later: "It was now clear that the entry port route was too dangerous and must be abandoned. There were five decks above the divers, supported by nothing in particular, and settlement was still going on, as we evidenced by loud noises and tremors which occasionally disturbed the men as, in darkness far inside the wreck, they struggled to squeeze themselves onwards through the narrow chinks."

Lieutenant-Commander Damant decided to blast his way down, deck by deck, to get at the missing ingots. It was an operation which was to eventually take seven years to complete, with a break of some years in between the first and last dives, during which £800,000 worth of gold was recovered.

Transferred to more urgent salvage work, Damant and his team finally returned to the Laurentic in 1918. They found the crater which they had blasted through the decks had collapsed. In a graphic account of the Laurentic operation, based on a rare interview with Damant, author James Dugan describes the scene. "The crater was sealed off with steel and plank decking, and underneath it was a compacted mass of rubbish, hundreds of smashed saloon chairs, mattresses, carpets, bedsprings, bathtubs, tiles and pannelling. Waterlogged debris of furniture was washing to and fro and it settled into a fresh excavation overnight. The mess was almost like cement, for now the sea was sweeping sand and

149

pebbles into the shattered Laurentic."

The mountain of assorted rubbish had to be cleared by hand, air-suction lines got clogged up with old mattresses and carpets. "In the dark, swirling water, they delved for gold with their bare hands. They could not feel a gold bar through gloves. They wore their finger-nails to stumps and finger-tips raw." The operation was finally completed in 1924 after more that 5,000 dives on the wreck. All but 25 of the 3,211 gold bars had been recovered.

While this dirty, dangerous and exhausting salvage feat was being carried out in the bitterly cold Atlantic, several hundred miles to the south-east, an American author was spending his free afternoons under far more attractive sea conditions.

Guy Gilpatric lived at Cap d'Antibes. He wrote during the morning and each afternoon went out with a small group of fellow enthusiasts to dive and spear fish. He had adapted a pair of flying-goggles, sealing them with putty, to enable him to see clearly and hunt more effectively. In 1938 Gilpatric published an account of his adventures in *The Compleat Goggler*, the first book on sport diving ever written.

The war came and with it personal tragedy for the American. When he learnt that his wife had an incurable cancer they decided to die together in a suicide pact. But the long, hot summers and the hundreds of dives which Gilpatric had enjoyed and written about so enthusiastically inspired others, amongst them Jacques Yves Cousteau, father of the modern aqualung.

One of the problems of diving with goggles was keeping the glass ports in the same plane to prevent the swimmer from seeing double. This was overcome by the development of the single-plate mask, designed by a retired French naval officer, Yves Le Prieur. What Le Prieur had overlooked was the simple idea of enclosing the nose within the mask, thus enabling the diver to equalise the pressure by exhaling and so prevent the mask from being flattened against his face. Le Prieur adopted a far more complicated arrangement, consisting of a rubber balloon attached to the mask by a tube which was squeezed to pump in more air. The break-through which seems so obvious today to have occurred to several different divers at the same time. The bulb-mask went into the museum and the equalising mask was born.

Leonardo da Vinci had sketched designs for swim fins in the 16th century, but it wasn't until 1933 that the first patents were taken out for the modern fin. By 1954 one company alone had sold two million pairs in the United States.

On a bleak December in 1942, a young French naval intelligence officer based at Marseille made his way through Occupied France to Paris. In a cluttered engineering work-shop, with the crash of German jackboots sounding on the cobble stoned street below, he outlined an idea which was to revolutionise skin-diving.

The officer was Jacques Yves Cousteau. Emile Gagnan the engineer he had come so urgently to Paris to meet, was an expert on industrial gas equipment.

An experienced diver, Cousteau combined his Intelligence duties with diving operations at Marseille. He and his companion Frederic Dumas carried out surveys and underwater clearance tasks mainly using a surface supplied diving device developed by a French engineer named Fernez. A pump fed air via a long tube and a duck-beak valve to a full face mask. This equipment was considered reasonably safe but accidents did happen. It was one such near tragedy involving Dumas that sent Cousteau hurrying up to Paris in search of a more efficient diving apparatus. In his book *The Silent World,* Cousteau recalls: "We were working on defences against broken pipes one day with Dumas seventy-feet down breathing from the Fernez pipe. I was in the tender watching the pipe, when I saw it rupture . . . I grabbed the pipe before it sank and reeled it in frantically ill with suspense. I could feel heavy tugs from below. Then Dumas appeared, red-faced and choking, his eyes bulging. But he was alive. He had locked his glottis in time and had then climbed the pipe hand-over-hand. We worked on the gear until it operated more reliably, but the pump could take us no further. It fastened us on a leash and we wanted freedom."

In Gagnan's workshop, Cousteau outlined his idea of a system which would supply the diver with just the right amount of air at the correct pressure, on demand. The engineer nodded and handed the startled officer a small, bakelite mechanism: "It is a demand valve I have been working on to feed cooking gas automatically into car engines," he explained; at that period of the war petrol shortage had made it necessary for cars to run on charcoal and natural gas.

A few weeks later Cousteau and Gagnan were ready to test a prototype valve in the river Marne. It worked perfectly while Cousteau was swimming horizontally, but as soon as he put his head down to dive the supply was shut off. If it was unable to provide a constant air supply in any and every position, the demand valve was useless. Bitterly disappointed they drove back to Paris. But even before they reached home the problem had been solved. "When I was standing up in the water the level of the exhaust was higher than the intake and that six-inch difference in pressure allowed the air to overflow," explained Cousteau. "When I stood on my head, the exhaust was six inches lower, suppressing the air flow. When I swam horizontally, the exhaust and intake were at the same pressure level and the regulator worked perfectly. We arrived at the simple solution of placing the exhaust as close as possible to the intake so that pressure variations could not disrupt the flow."

That simple modification solved their problem. In 1943 Cousteau and Dumas carried out more than 500 dives using the self-contained breathing apparatus. Skin-diving was born.

415 BC	Greek divers attack boom defence at Syracuse.
375 AD	Diving hoods with air pumps described.
1250	Sir Roger Bacon outlines an idea for air reservoirs for divers.
1472	Italians design a wooden submarine.
1500	Leonardo de Vinci sketches swim fins and designs for leather diving lungs.
1578	Submarine with hand operated ballast tanks developed by British inventor, William Bourne.
1660	Sir Robert Boyle carries out experiments using compressed air.
1690	Halley's diving bell goes down to 60 feet for ninety minutes.
1715	John Lethbridge invents leather diving suit.
1774	An hour long descent to 50 feet, off the French coast using a helmet diving suit fed by compressed air tank which was submerged with diver.
1790	Modern style diving bell used for construction of Ramsgate harbour.
1800	Nautilus, a hand propelled submarine, completes six hours' dive.
1815	A one hundred man submarine built in America.
1819	Siebe built a practical open helmet fed by compressed air.
1837	Siebe introduced prototype of modern diving helmet.
1862	El Actineo, a submarine using oxygen-regenerating life support system takes crew of ten on trips lasting five hours.
1864	War comes beneath the waves. Submarine David IV sinks USS destroyer Housatonic. Both craft lost.
1879	Independent lung, oxygen regenerating system, tested in England by Henry Fleuss.
1893	Louis Boutan, a Frenchman, takes world's first underwater photographs.
1899	Louis Boutan takes first underwater pictures using artificial lights.
1904	Helmet divers, Greek and Swedish, descend 195 feet to salvage wreck of destroyer.
1906	Damant dives to 200 feet during experiments conducted by Haldane.
1914	First underwater motion picture made by John Williamson, USA, from suspended chamber. A year later he made the world's first full length underwater feature "20,000 Leagues Under The Sea".

1917	Start of major salvage operations on Laurentic (to 1924) by team of divers under Damant.
1919	Theoretical use of helium mixes for deep dives proposed.
1924	Diving system using compressed air bottle and hand operated valve developed by Yves le Prieur, France. First experimental dives on oxygen-helium mix.
1924	Rubber fins developed.
1925	Experiments with underwater television.
1926	First artificial light colour pictures taken.
1928	Guy Gilpatric starts diving. First emergence of sport.
1930	Divers reach 344 feet on compressed air in UK. One man dies.
1932	Bathyshere dives to 2,170 feet. Spear-gun invented.
1933	First Sub-Aqua Club, the Bottom Scratchers of California, starts up.
1935	Amateur diving group Club des Sous-l'Eau founded in Paris by Yves Le Prieur. World's first diving club.
1937	Helium-oxygen dive to 420 feet in Lake Michigan.
1938	*The Compleat Goggler* by Guy Gilpatric published. World's first book on sport diving. Also in this year Hans Hass, Fredric Dumas, and Jacques Yves Cousteau form their diving teams.
1939	Cine film taken by automatic camera at depth of 4,200 feet.
1940	Cousteau and his associates take first underwater 35 mm movie film.
1941	Underwater combat teams using rebreathing equipment formed. Buster Crabbe and others protect ships at Gibraltar from Italian frogmen.
1943	Georges Comheines, Frenchman, makes aqua-lung dive to 166 feet. Not long afterwards Frédéric Dumas makes dive to 203 feet.
1945	Helmet dives using helium-oxygen mix to 528 feet by Swede.
1947	Cousteau's team dive to 297 feet.
1948	Dumas dives on compressed air to 307 feet. In this year the French Federation of Submarine Clubs is founded.
1949	Philippe Tailliez publishes decompression tables for successive dives using air.
1950	World's deepest underwater picture taken at 18,000 feet.
1951	H.M.S.Challenger locates bottom of Philippine Trench. In the same year underwater T.V. was used successfully to locate the missing submarine H.M. Affray.

1953	British Sub Aqua Club founded by Peter Small and Oscar Gugen.
1954	British Sub Aqua Club publish their handbook on diving safety for the first time. Their diving manual first published 1959.
1959	World Underwater Federation (C.M.A.S.) founded to control world wide diving activities.
1960	Jacques Piccard and Lt. Don Walsh dive seven miles in Trieste on 23rd January.
1960	Oldest wreck ever discovered is found off Turkey. Bronze age vessel some 3,000 years old.
1961	Swedish warship Vasa is raised after 333 years beneath the sea. One of the greatest triumphs of archaeological salvage ever achieved.
1962	Peter Small dies during simulated deep dive to 1,000 feet, conducted by Hannes Keller.
1962	Conshelf One. A 17 feet by 8 feet cylinder at a depth of 33 feet in the Mediterranean, off Marseille. Houses two men for one week.
1963	Conshelf II, a starfish shaped house in the Red Sea which houses five men for one month at 36 feet. Deeper cabin houses two men for a week at 96 feet.
1963	Loss of American atomic submarine Thresher.
1965	First simulated saturation dive with oxygen-helium to 650 feet for 48 hours.
1966	Sealab II, La Jolla, California. Underwater habitat in which three teams of ten men spent 15 days each at 205 feet. One diver, Commander Scott Carpenter, spent a month at depth.
1966	Experiments with breathing water by Dr Johannes Kylstra in the Netherlands.
1966	Conshelf III experiments off Cap Ferrat by Jacques Yves Cousteau. Six men lived for three weeks breathing mixture of 98 % helium, 2 % oxygen at 370 feet.
1966	Purisima, simulated descent to 650 feet by American company, Ocean Systems Inc. Dive lasted 48 hours.
1969	Tektite I. U.S. programme which put four scientists to 50 feet in habitat for sixty days in Great Lameshur Bay, St. John, Virgin Islands. During this period U.S. military experiments in training dolphins for various underwater tasks including aiding divers and attacking "enemy" frogmen. Use of dolphins exposed in book by Dr John Lilly, world's leading expert on dolphins.

154

1972   Project Flare, mobile underwater habitat which travelled
            around sea floor off coast of Florida during three month
            research project.

Key Facts About the Sea

The oceans of the world cover approximately 139,000,000 square miles or 72 % of the earth's surface. The average depth of the oceans is 12,420 feet. The Pacific Ocean is the largest with an area of 69,000,000 square miles, including adjacent seas. Its deepest point so far recorded is the Challenger Deep (measured by scientists aboard the survey vessel H.M.S. Challenger in 1951) at 36,200 feet, in the Marianas Trench. Its average depth is 13,000 feet.

The second largest ocean is the Atlantic with an area of 31,530,000 square miles. Its deepest point is the Puerto Rico Trench at 30,184 feet. Its average depth is 9,000 feet.

The third largest is the Indian Ocean with 28,350,000 square miles. Its deepest part lies in the Sunda Trench, 24,442 feet down. Its average depth is 12,000 feet.

If all the mountains and hills on earth were flattened out and land sank beneath the waves, oceans would totally cover the earth to a depth of 8,000 feet.

Further Reading

Man Explores the Sea. James Dugan. Hamish Hamilton, London, 1956. Now out of print. Exciting accounts of early dives and salvage operations, the development of underwater photography and scientific experiments.

The Silent World. Captain Jacques Yves Cousteau. Hamish Hamilton, London, 1953. A dramatic account by the father of the aqualung of his early dives and adventures.

Abyss. C. P. Idyll. Constable and Company, London, 1964. A first class description of life at great depths. Combines a scholarship with graphic writing.

Seven Miles Down. Jacques Piccard and Robert S. Dietz. The Scientific Book Club, London, 1963. Exciting account of the 1960 deep dive in Trieste. This dive is also fully described in National Geographic Magazine, August, 1960 (Vol. 118, No. 2).

The Bountiful Sea. Seabrook Hull. Sidgwick and Jackson, London, 1966. A good guide to many types of marine and submarine activities, research and biology in the deep.

Exploring the Secrets of the Sea. William J. Cromie. George Allen and Unwin, London, 1964. A highly readable history of man's exploration of the oceans.

We Come From the Sea. Hans Hass. Scientific Book Club, London, 1958. Interesting account of early diving and exploration by a pioneer of the sport.

The Underwater Book, The Second Underwater Book and *The World Underwater Book*. Books edited by Kendall McDonald and published by Pelham Books, London, 1970–1973. Accounts of different aspects of diving by a variety of authors, scientific experiments, wreck hunts, running a diving school and finning with sharks. Something for every enthusiast.

12

The Sea and Tomorrow

In the summer of 1969 I had the unusual experience of making a telephone call from a bubble of trapped air thirty feet down in the Mediterranean. In a "cottage-loaf" shaped habitat, some 9 feet long by 6 feet wide, made from rubberised fabric, I was able to take off my diving gear, breath the warm, humid air and realise what Jonah must have felt like when he was swallowed alive.

But for all its primitive design this habitat in Paradise Bay, off the coast of Malta, was an important milestone in the exploration of the sea. Compared with the American Tektite experiments of the same year, and Cousteau's Conshelf habitat 370 feet deep on the floor of the Mediterranean which had preceded both by three years, this brief, shallow water excursion was crude in the extreme. Its value was to show that cheap habitats are possible, the total cost of this student organised expedition was less than one twentieth of the development budget for one lavatory in the Russian habitat—and that ingenuity, determination and skill can produce valuable results. Brian Ray, one of the designers of the habitat and the life support systems it contained, told me then: "Underwater research is in the same position to aviation fifty years ago, we are at the bamboo and piano-wire stage where you discover the rules as you go along."

In the five years since I made that dive into the gin-clean waters of Paradise Bay, the technology of diving, encouraged by the need to exploit the industrial riches of the sea, has made a dramatic leap forward. Today we can predict with some certainty what tasks the divers of the year 2000 will be capable of performing and the type of sophisticated technology which will be available to them. The problems of nil visibility will be overcome, the physiological barriers to deep diving probably solved. Man will be living and working underwater for prolonged periods. There will be seabed oil and gas production plants, replacing the need for vulnerable surface platforms. There will be underwater research stations dotted around the Continental shelves, perhaps commercial farms where fish will be herded and cared for just like domestic animals on land. Men will have begun a detailed exploration of the Abyss, not only confined in submarines and diving bells but using flexible armoured suits which will enable explorers to walk the Abyss floor and life sample for examination. One such suit, capable of taking a man to 1300 feet has already been developed by a design team at a Farnborough factory. Looking like a heavy version of the moon walk suits, the armour, made from a magnesium based alloy, contains its own life support systems and a through the water communication set. The designers have managed to overcome the chief problem of earlier armoured suits, a seizing up of the joints under great pressure, by using the latest aluminium alloys.

As we saw in Chapter Three there are considerable physiological problems about breathing ordinary air under pressure. The nitrogen present causes the brain to hallucinate, and oxygen turns into a deadly poison. Equally serious is the long decompression time necessary after a really deep dive in order that the nitrogen is the body tissues can pass out again without forming bubbles.

One method of solving the first two problems is to use as little oxygen as possible in a special mixture of gases which consists only of oxygen and helium. The first successful simulated deep dive, to 650 feet for forty-eight hours, took place in 1965. A year later in the Conshelf III experiments, Jaques Yves Cousteau and his team spent three weeks at 370 feet breathing a mixture of 98% helium and 2% oxygen. Under experimental surface conditions volunteers have now "dived" to the equivalent of 1500 feet on this mixture.

Helium is an inert gas which has no effect on the brain although it is absorbed into the body tissues, 2.64 times faster than nitrogen so a long, slow return to normal atmospheric pressure is necessary.

What scientists are now searching for is a drug which will inhibit the speed at which helium is absorbed by the body tissues. At the present time the only chemicals which have any effect on the rate of absorption reduce it by such a small amount (20%) that they are no practical assistance to breaking through the deep dive barriers. Researchers believe that drugs will never be able to do more than double, or perhaps treble, the maximum depth at which a SCUBA diver can operate. This means that free-divers will one day be able to explore most of the Continental Shelf but never venture down into the Abyss.

Breathing helium has a strange side effect. Because the gas is less dense than air, the speed of sound is increased and this dramatically alters the pitch of the human voice. Divers sound like Donald Duck which may be amusing but poses a serious communications difficulty as the voice rapidly becomes unintelligible. During the Conshelf experiments Cousteau recalls: "Days would pass before the oceanauts could understand each other. They had to learn to speak slowly and succinctly, and to avoid high-pitched sounds." Sometimes the only way words could be understood was by recording the speakers on videotape: "If we did not understand the oceanaut's falsetto, we could watch his lip movements, gestures, and scribbles held up to the lens."

Now the problem of "Donald Duck" divers is a thing of the past thanks to an electronic decoder, developed by GEC-Marconi in conjunction with the Admiralty Research Laboratory, which stretches out the words, analysing each sound and reconstructing the essential parts of it at a slower speed. Early tests proved so successful that a Welshman was not only made intelligible, his accent came through the descrambler as well!

Various techniques for avoiding the use of helium at all have been proposed. One idea is to try and discover the perfect gas mix which would enable divers to breath oxygen safely under great pressure. So far little advance has been made in this direction.

A more startling idea is to flood the lungs completely and persuade our respiratory system to draw oxygen direct from liquid. It sounds like the ultimate method of drowning but considerable advances in this field have been made by Professor Johannes Kylstra at America's Duke University. Using laboratory animals and an oxygen saturated liquid he has proved that mamallian lungs are quite capable of adapting to liquid breathing. Although there have been considerable difficulties in removing the carbon dioxide, Professor Kylstra is confident that this problem can be overcome. According to a volunteer who had one lung flooded with liquid during experiments, there is no great discomfort in this technique. By the year 2000 such a system may be almost routine for dives below 300 feet.

The final method, which sounds even more alarming than breathing water, is to oxygenate the blood stream directly rather than via the lungs. An artery would be opened and fitted with a fine tube. Blood from the artery would then pass through a small box which introduced oxygen and removed carbon dioxide. The lungs would have to be filled with a liquid, to prevent the chest cavity being crushed by water pressure and would play no part in respiration. Outlining this system at the Oceans 2000 congress in London in 1973, Hannes Keller, a Swiss born scientist who was the first man to dive to 1000 feet, said that the depth limit with this system would be around 5000 feet.

Whichever system is finally adopted it is certain that divers operating at great depths will be working under pressure not only from the hundreds of tons of water pressing down on them but from the complexity of their equipment. In addition to sophisticated gas mixes or even more physiologically complicated breathing systems, they will have to operate electronic communications sets and manipulate a wide variety of survey and recording equipment. Coping with all this could well be too much for one man however carefully trained, and research is now concentrating on aiding divers in exactly the same way as a spaceman can be aided by land based experts. Ralph Shamlian, of Farallon Industries, believes that one answer may be a diving computer. On his arm the diver would wear a miniature computer with display unit connected to his gas cylinder. This would continually monitor the cylinder, using a sensor to transmit pressure as a voltage value to the panel where it would read out on digital tubes. The computer could work out decompression stages required against a pre-selected programme. On ascent the computer would indicate each depth at which a decompression stop had to be made and for how long a period. If the diver ascended too rapidly a warning buzzer would sound. By including a transmitter/receiver and throat microphone in the system the diver could have his progress monitored by a surface supervisor who might be in charge of several divers in the same area. A control board would indicate the exact state of cylinder pressure for each of the men under his command. In the event of a fault developing he would be able to bring the diver to the surface in sufficient time to carry out the necessary decompression stops.

Such instrumentation is probably no more that a couple of years away. The control of divers from the surface, via water borne signals which remove any need for umbilical links, will certainly be an important part of any commercial diving system of the future. At Fort Bovisand in Plymouth, I sat on the quayside next to a cathode-ray tube on which was being monitored the progress of a diver, swimming through poor visibility towards a target buoy in the harbour. A transmitter fitted to the target caused one blimp to appear in a static position on the screen. A second transmitter carried by the diver produced a moving dot. The quayside operator was able to guide the diver towards his target via a radio link in exactly the same way as an air traffic controller talks down a fog bound pilot.

Even without such a surface aid, equipment is available which enables divers to carry out accurate surveys and to go straight to targets even in nil visibility. A hand held and battery powered sonar locator will tell the diver his position in relation to a fixed beacon which may be planted on a wreck site, a well-head or a pipeline. Two lights flash on the locator when the diver is swimming towards the target, if only the left hand light flashes then the diver swims to the left until both light come on, if only the right hand light blinks then he swims to the right. At the present time the sonar beacon locator is a costly and relatively bulky instrument. Within a few years there is no doubt that it will be reduced to wristwatch size at a price all divers can afford. A rather similar system enables accurate measurements to be carried out for the survey work. The diver merely points the equipment at the target, to which a beacon has been fitted and reads off the distance as numbers on digital tubes.

So far I have discussed ideas and equipment which actually exist, if only as laboratory experiments and design prototypes. But beyond these realities, the exploration and exploitation of the sea could lead to systems which today seem like the wildest science fiction. Men farming whales, not only for their meat but for their milk, a cow whale produces about a ton a day. Gold and uranium, each cubic mile of sea contains about 25 tons of gold and 7 tons of uranium, harvested by means of specially developed marine organisms which would absorb the minerals selectively. Underwater power stations constructed to tap fast flowing submarine currents. All these ideas, put forward by Arthur C. Clarke, the writer who predicted communication satellites decades in advance

160

of their time, could be commonplace by the year 2000. Other writers and scientists dream of vast farms where divers would look after millions of fish, perhaps using trained dolphins as sub-aqua "sheep" dogs.

All of which suggests that man will survive the challenge of the sea. More open to question is whether the oceans can survive the confrontation with the human race. Much of the research now going on into deep diving techniques is financed by the military and industry. Both of them, many fear, have all the wrong sorts of vested interest in exploiting the deep. The military programmes are not merely alarming but actually work against an increase in man's knowledge since their programmes are often top secret. Many people were shocked by disclosures, made by Dr John Lilly the world's leading expert on dolphins, that these highly intelligent creatures had been trained in warfare. American scientists not only taught them to attack and kill frogmen, in order to protect port installations in Vietnam, but even experimented with using dolphins to mine enemy craft.

If the oceans are exploited as ruthlessly and destroyed as wantonly as many parts of earth have been, not all the blame will attach to the military and industry. The great increase in the popularity of the skindiver has already produced the ominous phrase "diver pollution".

On any warm weekend popular diving areas can become as congested beneath the waves as on the roads leading to them. Scores of divers will descend on a site, plunge in and surface an hour later loaded down with every type of flora and fauna from crayfish, which are at least eaten, to smaller specimens which often get dumped on the beach and left to rot. So ruthless has this pillaging been in some parts of the country that permanent damage has been caused to marine life. In October 1973 the British Sub Aqua Club put forward proposals for protecting the sea from the growth of the sport, to the Sports Committee of the World Underwater Federation. They asked for a Code of Diving Practice to be universally recognised by the 54 member nations. If adopted it would ban spear-fishing whilst using aqualungs and prohibit amateurs from selling their catches. It would prevent certain species, such as the grouper and other easily killed fish, from being hunted and enable individual countries to specify species they wanted to protect. It further proposed that some area should be designated as reserves and any taking of flora of fauna from them be strictly forbidden. They suggested that minimum size for catches should be agreed and strictly adhered to and that divers should observe the various codes of practice of professional fishermen and other water users. As far as the taking of specimens in general was concerned they asked that divers observe *moderation* in removing flora and fauna.

Although the mood of the congress was for conservation and the proposals extremely modest, some delegates still felt that Mediterra-

161

nean countries would violently oppose the clauses relating to spear-fishing.

In June of the same year Jacques Cousteau, the father of modern skin-diving, resigned from the Presidency of the World Underwater Federation in protest against their support on spear-fishing. "The reason I stayed so long with this organisation is because I thought that by appropriate action this confederation would progressively steer the passion and interest of divers to non-hunting activities," he said. "It has been a failure."

If Cousteau is right then the future of diving in inshore waters is a gloomy one and our children may fin endlessly over barren rocks and lifeless sea floors where the pillaged wilderness bears grim testimony to man's ability as the world's most accomplished predator.

I hope and believe that this is too black a picture. Legislation may help, indeed a framework of laws and prohibitions is probably essential to deter the greedy from their more vulnerable trophies. But laws are hard to enforce. In the Mediterranean there are teams of sub-aqua policemen whose job it is to uphold the stringent regulations protecting historic wreck sites. The frequently poor visibility around our shores could make such supervision extremely difficult.

The best answer I believe is to be found less in the law as in education. The majority of divers will probably agree that ignorance as much as malice lies at the root of much destruction. "The sea is so vulnerable and helplessly endangered today," says Jacques Cousteau. "I am not just speaking of the Mediterranean, I am speaking of everywhere."

The future of the sea is closely linked to man's future on this planet. We need the oceans to feed growing populations, as a source of energy and mineral wealth, and, for the sport of diving, as the most exciting, awe-inspiring and fascinating playground on earth.

162

Appendix 1

First Aid

Every diver should have a knowledge of simple first aid, especially artificial respiration. Best resuscitation method, since it is easy to learn and you are able to use it even in the confined space of a diving boat, is the expired air or "kiss of life" technique. This should be carried out in the following manner.

1. Lie victim flat with head turned to one side. Make sure there is no obstruction in the mouth or throat.

2. Tilt the head back to arch the neck and make sure the airway is clear.

3. Close the nostrils of the victim with two fingers. Take a deep breath and place your mouth over the victim's, sealing his mouth with your lips. Exhale deeply. If a gurgling sound is heard there is an obstruction in the airway. Check to make sure there is no debris or vomit in the mouth. Make sure the head is tilted right back.

4. If the victim's chest rises the airway is clear. Breath at the rate of about ten exhalations per minute. Breath deeply. Continue until the victim recovers or a doctor pronounces death.

Cuts and Grazes

May be more serious than any originally looked or felt underwater. A well equipped diving boat should carry a standard first aid kit. Apply a clean dressing after cleaning the wound in water and applying antiseptic cream. Even if no first aid kit is carried in the diving boat, each diver ought to have a tin of sticking plasters in his kit-bag.

If there is a serious injury with considerable blood loss it will be necessary to stop the flow and get the patient to land as rapidly as possible. Blood loss from a leg or arm injury can be reduced by raising the injured limb and applying a sterile bandage. If no dressings are available, clean cloth can be used. A tourniquet should not be applied as it can cause severe damage. Apply pressure on a sterile dressing placed over the wound to stop the bleeding.

Burns and scalds

The pain can be stopped by keeping air away from the injury which may have been caused by dry heat (burn) or hot liquid (scald). Place under cold water tap or immerse in clean water. Apply clean, preferably sterile, dressing to exclude air.

163

Heart stopped or irregular

In cases of fresh water drowning particularly, the heart may have stopped functioning or the heart-beat may be irregular. In order to stimulate or restart the heart pressure should be applied at the lower end of the breast bone. The pressure should be made with the heel of the hand, one hand placed over the other to increase the pressure. Press hard enough to push down the breast bone (sternum) by about one and half inches. Pressure should be applied once a second. It may accompany mouth to mouth resuscitation.

Hypothermia

Cover with blankets or coats, give warm drinks and food. Do not give any alcohol.

Sea Urchin Spines

These can all too easily enter the hand or foot when making a beach dive or exploring rocks. The spines are painful and may produce a septic wound. If they are too deep to remove with tweezers bind the affected area in a dressing soaked in Epsom Salts. This will draw out the spine in a couple of days.

In general

After a serious accident the victim may be extremely shocked. Shock is made worse by bleeding, anxiety, exposure and exhaustion. Stop bleeding as rapidly as possible. It may help to lie the victim flat with the head in a slightly lower position to ensure a good supply of blood to the brain. Do not cover excessively as too much heat may make shock worse, simply keep warm and protect from exposure.

Appendix 2

Seamanship Hints
Tides: There are three well-defined tides.

1. Semi-diurnal—experienced all around Britain and western Europe as well as in other parts of the world. Sea level oscillates between high and low water twice in each 24 hour period. The *RANGE* of the tide is the difference in sea level at high and low water. The interval between high and low water is called the *DURATION* of the tide. Tidal *Range* can vary considerably, *Duration* is approximately 6 hours. Once every fifteen days SPRING tides occur when the moon and sun combine to create the greatest *Range*. These occur about $1\frac{1}{2}$ days after the full moon and new moon. Also every fifteen days throughout the year *Neap* tides occur. These are caused by the lunar and solar forces working at right angles to each other. *Neap* tides have the least *Range* with the highest low water levels and the lowest high water levels.
2. *Diurnal Tides*: These are experienced in the tropics mainly. There is one low water and one high water a day and the range is small.
3. *Mixed Tides*: Found on the Pacific Coast of North America and the Australian coast. There are two highs and two lows each day but differences in the heights or successive high waters and low waters.

Tide Calculations
Each day newspapers print the time of high water at London Bridge. A table of tidal constants obtainable from Marine suppliers allows a calculation to be made based on London Bridge High Tide. Simply add or subtract the times given from London Bridge High Tide. Local papers in Seaside towns print tables giving the tides in their area.

Navigational Marks
Lights, buoys and sound are used to give warning or fix positions at sea. The sports diver who only spends a few hours not many miles from land and returns before dark has no real need to memorise the different types of light marks, but knowledge of the following types of buoy may be useful.

Landfall and Fairway
Shape: Usually tall pillar buoys. May have conical superstructures.

Colour: Black and white or red and white vertical stripes.
Lights: Quick flashing or flashing when fitted.

Wreck Buoys:
Shape: May be can, conical or spherical.
Colour: Green and white on side.
Light: Green flashing.

Outfall Buoys
Colour: Yellow and black in horizontal or vertical stripes. May also mark area used for dumping by dredgers.

Danger Area Buoys
Will show red flags by day, red fixed or flashing lights by night. May mark military gunnery target area.

Submarine Mining Buoys
Colour: Green and white horizontal stripes or checkboard pattern.

Mooring Buoys
Colour: Black normally and usually can or cylindrical in shape.

Flags
When divers are down the blue and white diving flag A should be hoisted. Flags should be clearly displayed and kept flying so long as divers are in the water. However in these days of widespread ignorance amongst small boat users total reliance should not be placed in the flag alone, a look-out must be kept to warn off power boats and others.

Weather
Forecasts should always be obtained before planning a sea trip. Wind Force is measured along an international scale, the Beaufort Scale, which is reproduced below. Forecasts issued to shipping by the BBC divide the sea around Britain into areas which may be seen from the map below.

Emergency
Before setting out to sea on a diving expedition you will be well advised to notify the local coastguards of your intention and approximate return time. In this way prompt action can be taken if you are overdue. If you do this, however, you must not overlook notifying the coastguards of your safe return or an unnecessary search may be mounted. Distress flares should be carried on every sea diving expedition. If you are without flares set fire to some old rags and wave a make-shift alarm signal, for example, a shirt fixed to an oar.

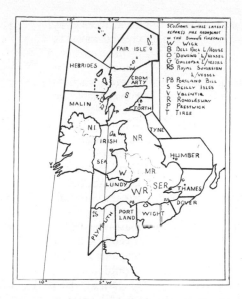

Fig. 9. The main sea areas around our shores used in shipping forecasts.

Nautical Terms and Measurements

Cable. cable is one tenth of a nautical mile. In practice 200 yards.
Nautical Mile: In practice 6,080 feet. Theoretically the length of one minute of arc measured along the meridian.
Knot: A nautical mile per hour. One knot is equal to 1.7 feet per second.
Fathom: Six feet.
Wind-Speed: Can be expressed either in knots or miles per hour.
      Direction. Taken as the direction *from which* the wind blows.

Beaufort Scale

Beaufort Number	Description of Wind	Effect of Wind on land	Speed in knots
0	Calm	Smoke rises vertically	Less than one
1	Light air	Smoke drifts wind vanes do not more	1–3
2	Light breeze	Wind felt on face. Leaves rustle	4–6
3	Gentle breeze	Leaves and twigs in motion. Flags begin to move.	7–10
4	Moderate breeze	Raises dust and blows scraps of paper along.	11–16

167

5	Fresh breeze	Small trees sway, crested wavelets form on sheltered waters	17–21
6	Strong breeze	Large branches move, telephone lines whistle	22–27
7	Moderate gale	Whole trees move, hard to walk against wind Head for harbour. Go into pub.	28–33
8	Fresh gale	Breaks twigs off trees	34–40
9	Strong gale	Slates moved. Structural damage may occur. Stay in pub!	41–47
10	Whole gale	Seldom experienced on land	48–55
11	Storm	Widespread damage Safest in pub	56–65
12	Hurricane	Pub probably destroyed. Take up golf or emigrate	Over 65

Appendix 3

Glossary of technical terms used in Chapters Five and Six.

CdS Meter: In this system light falling on a sensitive cell varies its resistance to an electric current supplied by a small battery. Because there is always power present to overcome the inertia of the hair-spring, which restrains the measuring needle, CdS systems are able to make readings at lower light levels than selium cell meters (see below).

Chromatic Aberration: A loss of image definition caused by light rays of different wavelengths being focused at slightly different points. This is especially apparent when using very wide-angle lenses underwater and shooting through a flat port.

Depth of Field: Those parts of a subject, in front of and behind the actual point of focus which are sharply defined on the photograph. The smaller the f-stop used the greater is the depth of field.

Film Speed: A rating given to each type of film by the manufacturers. Three systems are used. The ASA (American Standards Association). The BS (British Standards) and the DIN (German Standards) numbers. The speed is expressed by one or more of these codes followed by a number. The higher the number the faster the film, that is the less light it needs to produce a correctly exposed negative or colour transparency. For example, Kodak Tri-X rated at ASA 400 is twice as fast as Kodak High Speed Ektachrome rated as ASA 160.

Flash Factor: A figure supplied with bulbs or electronic guns to enable the correct f-stop to be calculated. Flash factors vary with the speed of film being used, the faster the film the higher the factor. To find the f-stop simply divide the subject—light distance into the factor: i.e. Flash factor 160, distance 20 feet, f-stop required f-8.

Focal length: The focal length of a lens is the distance from a determined point within the lens system, (the nodal point) at which it forms a sharp image of an object at infinity. For example, a 50 mm lens will form a sharp image of a distant object at a distance of 50 mm. A lens is said to be normal if it is being used to cover a negative area whose diagonal is more or less equal to the focal length. For example, the diagonal of a 6 cm × 6 cm negative is approximately 8 cm and so an 8 cm, or 80 mm lens is said to be the normal or standard focal length for that negative size. If we make a lens cover a negative area whose diagonal is much larger than its focal length, the lens is said to be wide-angle. For example, a 50 mm lens is standard on 35 mm, a 24 mm lens is very wide angle, while a 135 mm lens, a focal length longer than the diagonal, is long focus.

Grain Size: Photographic images are made up of grains of silver. The denser the silver formation the darker that part of the image. Forced development or sudden changes in temperature during processing can cause the individual silver grains to clump making them more obvious in the final print or transparency and leading to loss of image definition.

Pin-Cushion Distortion: Sides of a square object appear to bow outwards. This is due to the outer portions of the picture being magnified more than the central portions. An opposite effect, when a square appears to bow inwards, is known as barrel distortion.

Selenium Cell Meter: A light meter which works because light falling on the cell produces an amount of electricity in direct proportion to the amount of light present. Selenium meters tend to be slightly less sensitive than CdS meters but they need no additional power source and can be completely sealed in perspex cases.

Visible Spectrum: Light is a minute part of the electromagnetic spectrum. Waves with very long wavelengths are used to transmit radio signals, as the wavelengths get shorter we feel them as heat. When they shorten still further they stimulate the eye and are then known as the *visible spectrum*. The spectrum is measured in angstrom units Å.

The visible spectrum extends from 4000 to 7000 Å. The longest wavelengths are those forming red light (6000 Å to 7000 Å) then comes green (5000 Å to 6000 A) and finally blue-violet (4000 Å to 5000 Å). Waves shorter than 4000 Å form ultra-violet light which is invisible to the human eye although it can be used, as can infra-red at the opposite end of the visible spectrum, for taking photographs. White light is a mixture of various wavelengths and contains all the colours in the spectrum.

Index

172

174